CRISIS MANUAL

for Christian Schools and Youth Workers

Sandy J. Austin

How to Prepare for and Handle Tragedy

BEACON HILL PRESS
OF KANSAS CITY

Copyright 2007
by Sandy J. Austin and Beacon Hill Press of Kansas City

ISBN-13: 978-0-8341-2310-6
ISBN-10: 0-8341-2310-X

Printed in the
United States of America

Cover Design: J.R. Caines
Interior Design: Sharon Page

Library of Congress Cataloging-in-Publication Data

Austin, Sandy.
   Crisis manual for Christian schools and youth workers : how to prepare for and handle tragedy / Sandy J. Austin.
      p. cm.
   Includes bibliographical references (p.   ).
   ISBN-13: 978-0-8341-2310-6 (pbk.)
   ISBN-10: 0-8341-2310-X (pbk.)
   1. School crisis management—United States—Handbooks, manuals, etc. 2. Church schools—United States—Administration—Handbooks, manuals, etc. I. Title.

   LB2866.5.A87   2007
   371.7'13—dc22

                                                                2007002009

10 9 8 7 6 5 4 3 2 1

DEDICATION

This book is dedicated to Betsy Thompson

Betsy, you have comforted so many school personnel and children who were experiencing grief. You have taught me almost everything I know about crisis response. Thank you for your tireless work to save and heal lives.

CONTENTS

ACKNOWLEDGEMENTS

I would like to express my appreciation to the staff at Beacon Hill Press of Kansas City and Barefoot Ministries—especially Bonnie Perry, Judi Perry, and Jeff Edmondson—for seeing the need to address the difficult topic of crisis response. Countless lives will be touched and saved as a result of your vision.

I am thankful to my mom, Dora Austin, who believes in me and has spent many hours reviewing the manuscript while I was up late working on the book.

Thanks to Annie Willis and Bryan Hull for their help in getting my manuscript ready to send to the publisher. And a big thank you to my writing mentors, Marlene Bagnull, Virelle Kidder, and Linda Evans-Shepherd.

And last but certainly not least, thank you to the many people who supported me in prayer through writer's block and exhaustion. I pray that God will richly bless you.

INTRODUCTION

April 20, 1999, is forever etched in my mind. As a second-year school counselor, I, along with other mental health workers in our school district, were asked to report to Columbine High School in response to a shooting at the school. I spent the next week counseling students and families struggling with the realities of the tragedy. The following summer, I spent two days each week counseling those who were still struggling.

As a member of crisis response teams, I have responded to the devastating blows of the deaths of both students and staff members over the years. Colorado was again recently touched by a school tragedy with the unique twist of an adult gunman dropping in off the street, and I was asked to help the school and the church community with the healing process. Over the years I have served as a consultant for various schools and churches as they dealt with the aftermath of crisis.

The information I share here comes from the lessons I learned through my experiences as a school counselor, crisis team member, president of the Colorado School Counselor Association, part-time youth director, and other positions

I've held in churches and ministries caught in the turmoil of tragedy.

This book will give you tools you can use to prepare for crisis when—not if—it occurs. If God has called you to a position of leadership, He will equip you for the responsibilities of your position through resources, information, and qualified people.

I applaud you for picking up this book. It may very well save you from trying to reinvent the wheel when effective crisis response depends on you. God bless you in your service for Him.

1 THE NEED FOR A CRISIS PLAN

As the church van made new tracks down the quiet road in the glistening snow, the students' voices rang through the night with the praise songs "Shout to the Lord" and "Awesome God," sounds to put a smile on the face of God. The youth group slowly made its way home from the retreat on a spiritual high that would last forever—or so they thought.

The words crashed to a dead silence as the van began to tailspin and slide toward a ravine. A tire clipped the curb and tipped the van into a roll. Crunching glass flew, and the sound of twisting metal pierced the night air as the vehicle rolled and rolled down the ravine, finally landing upright in the snow. The blaring horn aroused Jesse from his daze.

"Seth, are you OK?" Jesse shouted, unbuckling his seatbelt and reaching over to pull Seth off the steering wheel. No response. "Oh, no—the other van doesn't know!" Jesse said, gasping. "Are you guys OK?" Jesse yelled to the six middleschoolers in the van. Amid groans and whines, he saw slight movements among the six.

Jesse pulled out his cell phone to call people in the other van. Nothing—no reception. Just then headlights blinded Jesse as a truck pulled up next to them.

□ □ □

"Dr. Atkinson, Johnny was just jumped outside by some kids from Westside High!" Cindy screamed as she ran into the office. "They bashed his head in, and he's bleeding all over!"

"I brought my kid to this Christian school to get away from these problems," a mother waiting in the office declared. Several office staff ducked into other offices to spread the word.

"Where is he, Cindy?" Dr. Atkinson said as he ran with her out of the office. They sprinted across the street to Johnny's side as he lay unconscious in the gutter next to his car. Hysterically, Cindy chatted endlessly as Dr. Atkinson tried to help Johnny.

Students streamed from the school after they heard the sirens of the emergency vehicles rushing to the scene. Three students dashed across the street. An ambulance veered to miss them as it careened around the corner. People in neighboring homes stared from their front yards. Mothers from down the block wheeled their babies in strollers to see the commotion. Chaos ensued as teachers stood together talking while their students searched for friends—crying and hugging each other, fearing the worst.

I Don't Think We're in Kansas Anymore

As Dorothy said to Toto, "I don't think we're in Kansas anymore." Today we've learned that working with young people is not simply fun and games while trying to instill good morals and behavior in them. We can't continue in youth work as we always have in the past. Life happens, and the harsh reality of our world today means we're not immune to difficulties the rest of the world faces. It is not a question of *if* a tragedy will strike under our watch but *when*.

As leaders working with youth, we're responsible to do all we can to be as fully prepared as possible. We must take advantage of every opportunity to equip ourselves to be as competent as possible in our positions. No one can use the excuse anymore that he or she didn't know a crisis plan was needed. The chance of a tragedy of Columbine High School magnitude is unlikely, but there are many other types of situations that can have a crippling effect on your young people.

Situations similar to the ones mentioned can happen at any time. In those examples a crisis plan was not in place, so immediately many things transpired that heightened the severity of the crises. For example, in the first situation with the youth group traveling home from a winter retreat, one of the first things their crisis plan should have mandated was for the two vans to travel close enough to be always visible to each other. That would not have stopped what happened, but it would have prevented many of the ensuing problems. The other van carried able-bodied people who could call 911, flag down other vehicles on the road, help with the injured, and so on.

In the crisis at the Christian school, a crisis plan would have assigned jobs to everyone and curtailed the chaos that resulted. Upon hearing the news, the office staff would have immediately focused its attention on individual responsibilities assigned within the plan. That would have created an orderly response to the crisis at hand while de-escalating the fear of the staff, parents, and students.

Problems can also arise when we don't adhere to the crisis plan we have or when we get lax in carrying it out. An example of not carrying out the plan recently occurred at a school in Missouri where several deaths occurred throughout the year. At the end of the year another student died. The administration was so weary from the other crises that they simply decided not to acknowledge the death by making an announcement to the students or by sending a letter home, simply thinking it would be too much for the students to handle.

They thought wrong. Instead, school administrators faced an onslaught of accusations from the community of incompetence, insensitivity, and even prejudice. So in the aftermath of the death, rather than dealing with a grieving student body, staff, and community, the leaders also had to deal with the backlash of the accusations. We all know what a litigious society we live in. This is an enormous issue when it comes to crisis response, and having a well-planned crisis response can prevent a lot of headaches. We list some important resources for you in the "Recommended Resources" section in the back of the book.

Selection of Crisis Team Members

The selection and placement of crisis team members may be the most important decisions you'll make in your leadership position. If all team members understand their roles on the team, there will be less chance of someone usurping the main leader's authority. All phases of the crisis response will be covered, because all team members are accountable for carrying out their own areas of responsibility. Team members must be committed to supporting, backing up, confronting, and covering for each other. That's why the selection of people on the team is crucial to its effectiveness.

It's recommended to have two people who hold the same staff positions serving on the crisis team or serving as backup. If one becomes ineffective or unable to perform his or her responsibilities, then the other team member can fill the gap. All crisis team members must be somewhat familiar with the responsibilities of the other members. With each crisis, certain positions will have added responsibility or pressure, and those people may need extra help or backup. The functioning of the crisis team will depend on the crisis. There should be a minimum of ten people on the team, not including backups. We'll discuss this later in the chapter.

Often outside the regular workday, a church or school will be notified of a crisis involving one of its young people. In that case the crisis team may be asked to meet as soon as possible or early the next morning. This will give the team time to think through its response and make plans accordingly. At other times when a crisis occurs, immediate response is needed before the crisis team can meet. Steps are taken at a moment's notice, and decisions are made as the crisis unfolds. Usually in these cases the crisis team won't be able to meet until later in the day.

Crisis team members must be people who are respected in their assigned positions as well as able to think quickly on their feet. They must be team players who will advocate for the best interests of the youth group or school. They must be able to uphold confidentiality. Their faith and dependence on God must be evident, because they may get into situations in which they're at their wits' end and will need to depend on God alone for strength and wisdom in dire circumstances. Team members should also have good communication skills to effectively deliver information to all parties during a crisis. One requirement for all crisis team members is to be certified in CPR and have first-aid training.

Crisis teams will look a little different for youth groups than they do for schools. There are many similarities, but there are also some noticeable differences. We've named positions with titles that can be used for both churches and schools. We'll discuss youth group crisis teams first.

Youth Group Crisis Teams

Youth Director. Since the youth group is part of a larger church, there are probably leaders who hold a higher position in the church than the youth director. (We'll use the term "youth director" to represent all those in this position, which would include youth directors, youth pastors, and so on.)

Discussion between the senior pastor, the youth director, and others who hold lay leadership positions with the church, such as elders, deacons, board members, and so on, is necessary to decide who will be the point person on the crisis team as it pertains to the youth group. Typically this is the youth director, since there will be many times the youth group is away from the church when a crisis occurs. The church should have a crisis team for the church as a whole, which the senior pastor/official will typically head. So it follows that the youth director will be in charge of the youth group crisis team.

Church Leaders. Two church leaders should also be on the youth group crisis team. This might be associate pastors, elders, deacons, board members, or other leaders within the church depending on its size. These leaders will support the youth director with needed resources and will communicate with others in leadership what's needed during the crisis. These leaders will fill specific roles, which we'll discuss in the next chapter.

Youth Workers/Volunteers. All other adults who are on the youth group staff should be on the crisis team. If you have a large youth group with many volunteers, it may not be necessary to have all volunteers on the crisis team, but they need to be made aware of the crisis plan so they can be backups for crisis team members.

Secretary. If you have a large youth group with a secretary on the youth staff, he or she should be on the crisis team. If you don't have a secretary, then someone needs to be designated as the recorder of all information and documentation. That person should have a backup who can cover in the secretary's absence and understand the workings of the crisis team. There should also be a filing system established for crisis forms and materials that is accessible and easy to understand for anyone needing information quickly.

Parents. Two parents should be on the crisis team in an auxiliary role. These should be parents of students who are active and well respected in the youth group. They should be supporters of youth group activities and active in the church themselves. These parents should be from different families instead of a couple from one family. They can be married or single. It would help if they have some experience in crisis intervention personally or through their jobs, but it's not necessary. These parents must be highly respected among the parents of the students in the youth group.

Student Leaders. Two students should be on the crisis team in an auxiliary role. These should be students in the oldest grade the youth group covers (for example, 12th-graders in a high school youth group). They must have good character and be as mature as can reasonably be expected in that age-group. They should be students who have proved to be dependable and trustworthy and who will uphold the strictest confidentiality. They should be respected by peers and adults alike and be positive role models for all students in the youth group.

Other Possible Crisis Team Members. You may want other members on the team, which will depend on the size of the youth group and community, the number of schools your youth group members represent, and so on. If teachers or staff members at schools within your community attend your church, you may want to invite them to be on the team. They may have valuable input on how to work with the schools in your area in case of a crisis. If your church has someone who works in the emergency or medical profession, it may be beneficial to have that person on the crisis team or to use him or her as a consultant if possible. Other positions may be added depending on the needs of your group.

Christian School Crisis Teams

Principal. The principal will lead the crisis team and will facilitate the crisis team meetings and guide the activation of the crisis plan. This is the point person throughout the crisis. Once informed of the crisis, the principal confers with the key people in determining the initial stages of the response—collecting and confirming details of the crisis, notifying and gathering the crisis team, and so on. Other responsibilities of the principal will be discussed in greater detail in the second chapter.

Other Administrators. Crisis team members are determined by the size of the school. It's good to have all school administrators on the team, but there may be times when the team must meet when some of the administrators are unable to attend. A backup leader must be designated in the event the principal is unavailable during the meetings. The backup leader or point person should be an administrator if possible.

Counselors. If the school has counselors or other mental health workers, there should be at least one on the crisis team—preferably two if the school has at least two on staff. These team members are valuable in assessing the mental health needs of the students, staff, and parents. They can coordinate efforts in the prevention, intervention, and "postvention" (after the crisis) stages. These crisis team members play key roles in helping the school recover in the aftermath of the crisis while helping the school return to normal functioning as soon as possible. If the school does not have counselors to fill both positions, then recruit a staff member who understands the mental health needs of young people.

Teachers. The two teachers on the crisis team must be well respected by other faculty and staff. They will be the voice for the teachers in monitoring the climate of the school and will be a direct link in determining student and faculty needs. They must be experienced teachers who understand teaching and the pressures inherent in the profession. They must be team players who can think clearly during stressful situations.

Head Custodian. The person in charge of maintenance for the school must also be on the crisis team. This person has valuable knowledge of the layout of the school, inherent hazards of the building, and where shutoffs of electricity, gas, water, and other utilities are located. This is crucial information for emergency service personnel who may be called to the school. If there is not another custodian to serve as backup in this capacity, choose an administrator or another staff member with knowledge in these areas.

Principal's Secretary. It's important that the principal's secretary serve on the crisis team. He or she will be responsible for keeping detailed records of crisis team meetings and documentation of the crises. As with other positions, there must be a designated backup person who can fill in for the secretary, and this person must be kept up to date with all information regarding the crisis team, crisis plan, and so on. It may be necessary to include the backup person in all meetings. It's crucial to have a filing system that's easy to follow for anyone needing information in a time of crisis.

Parents. There's been debate regarding having parents on a school crisis team, because they may not be able to remain as neutral in crisis situations as school professionals when their children or children's friends could be involved in the emergency at hand. It may be best to have two parents serve in auxiliary roles—not attending crisis team meetings but serving in an advisory capacity. These parents can be the voice of the parents of the school and can offer input to crisis team members as the need arises. They can also be the spokespersons for the school/parent organization if the school has one.

Students. As with parents, it typically is not advisable to have students on the crisis team. Students typically do not possess the maturity to handle the stress of dealing with severe crisis. Choosing two students to serve in an auxiliary role would be the most effective way to get feedback as to the needs of the students.

Other Possible Members. Depending on the size of the

school, you may want to include other members. If you have a large school or are in the position to have security personnel, those persons should be on the crisis team. If your school is one of several schools in a district, you may have a designee from the district involved on the team. If your school district has multiple levels (elementary, middle school, high school), you'll need to have each level represented, and it will depend on the team's preferences as to how many teachers you have on the team—one or two per level. The same goes for other members. Some schools have community medical or emergency personnel on the crisis team. This may not produce the best results, because often those individuals are not as immediately available as school personnel since they work off-site. It's good for key members of the crisis team to meet with community personnel in the prevention or "postvention" stage to include their input in the crisis plan. During a crisis, these people may be available and can advise at the scene of the emergency, but often they can't be readily available for a crisis team meeting. An auxiliary position may be recommended for these people too.

Again, the addition of other crisis team members will depend on the size of the school, size of the community, and the community resources available. In a small community, more members may need to be involved. These decisions must be made by the crisis team as a whole after considering the pros and cons of having extra people on the team.

As you can see, the selection of members for the crisis team takes a lot of consideration and forethought. This is the first step in creating a crisis plan. The next step is to consider the types of crises the plan will address.

Situations Your Crisis Plan Should Address

Countless crises are possible. Efforts should be made to address as many as possible in the crisis plan. Here we'll consider only a few. It will take time for your crisis team to think through the many possible scenarios your group may encounter, but following is a list to get you started:

- Vehicle emergencies away from the premises, such as accidents, running out of gas, flat tires, engine, or mechanical problems
- Injuries or illnesses while on trips
- Deaths on trips
- Fires in the building
- Lockdowns
- Earthquakes
- Tornadoes
- Floods
- Hazardous spills
- Blizzards
- Kidnappings on mission trips or class trips
- Travel emergencies, such as passport issues, accidents, missed flights, missing members
- Church or school shooting or violent intruder

These are some of the crises youth groups and schools potentially face. You'll want to start with the most likely crises that could occur with your group and list the steps needed to respond to those crises. This process will take a lot of time. You probably already have plans in place for many of these scenarios. Begin compiling the information in an orderly fashion for your crisis manual. A sample format is shown in chapter three. For information on emergency situations you may not be familiar with, refer to the "Recommended Resources" section at the back of this book.

As you can see by all the crises listed in this chapter, a crisis plan should cover a multitude of situations. The selection of crisis team members is vital to the effectiveness of the plan, because each crisis will be different, and the members must be able to adapt to all possible scenarios. We have briefly discussed who should be on the crisis team, but now we will more thoroughly cover each member's responsibilities.

2 CRISIS TEAM RESPONSIBILITIES

Each member of your crisis team will have vital responsibilities in carrying out the crisis plan. Let's revisit the examples in the opening chapter and see how events might have unfolded differently if a crisis plan had been in place.

Trip Home from the Retreat

As the church van made new tracks down the quiet road in the glistening snow, the students' voices rang through the night with the praise songs "Shout to the Lord" and "Awesome God," sounds to put a smile on the face of God. The youth group slowly made its way home from the retreat on a spiritual high that would last forever—or so they thought. The words crashed to a dead silence as the van began to tailspin and slide toward the ravine.

"Chris, the other van is sliding!" Maria shrieked as she stared into the rearview mirror.

"Slow down and pump the brakes to a stop," Chris instructed Maria, twisting his body to witness the horrifying scene as the van behind them careened down into the ravine.

Crunching glass flew, and twisting metal pierced the night air as the van rolled and rolled down the ravine, finally landing upright in the snow.

Panicking, Chris yelled, "Hurry up and stop this van!" Finally it rolled to a halt. Taking a deep breath, Chris climbed out of the van and continued: "OK, Bryan—call 911. Crisis members, do your jobs."

"I can't believe it—no service!" Bryan shouted after dialing.

Handing Bryan her cell phone, Sarah said, "Here—try mine."

Bryan dialed frantically. "Please help us!" he exclaimed to the operator. "We've had an accident!" Shaking and shivering, Bryan gave the details over the phone.

"I've got the first-aid kit!" Alicia yelled as she followed Chris and other youth group members toward the wrecked van. Derek guided Maria as she slowly backed her van to the area of the road adjacent to the disabled van.

"Seth, are you OK?" Chris blurted out, throwing the van door open and gently pulling him off the blaring horn. Seth was unconscious.

"Jesse, Jesse!" Alicia cried through her tears, fearing the worst for her new husband, arousing Jesse from his daze.

Others in the van began to stir except for Jenny, Twila, and Jared in the back seat.

"Can we open the back door to get some blankets?" Chris asked. "Don't move anyone until the paramedics get here."

Six girls huddling next to the van sobbed for their friends.

"The door's jammed!" Jeff yelled from the back of the van.

"Girls, run to the other van and get the blankets," Chris said, directing them in the midst of their cries.

Hearing the sound of sirens, Chris asked, "Who's flagging down the paramedics?" *God, please get them here on time,* he prayed.

"Derek is," Jeff answered.

Just then, headlights illuminated the van as the ambulance pulled off the road.

Innocence Shattered at a Christian School

"Dr. Atkinson, Johnny was just jumped outside by some kids from Westside High!" Cindy screamed as she ran into the office. "They bashed his head in, and he's bleeding all over!"

"I brought my kid to this Christian school to get away from these problems," Mrs. Jamison, a mother waiting in the office, declared. Christy, the attendance secretary, motioned for the mother to come into her office to help calm her down.

"Julie, call 911, then call Johnny's parents," Dr. Atkinson said to his secretary. "Where is he, Cindy?" He ran with her out of the office.

"Operator, we have an emergency at our school," Julie explained as she made the call. Then, after making the call to Johnny's mother, she headed out to the scene.

Julie saw Dr. Atkinson and Cindy at Johnny's side as he lay unconscious in the gutter next to his car. Dr. Atkinson spoke gently, trying to wake Johnny.

Back in the office, Christy tried to reassure the mother. "Mrs. Jamison, we don't know what's happened, but we'll take care of the situation. Christian schools are not immune to such problems." Christy kept the mother in her office until her child came down to meet her. She then asked the mother to remain in the office until the situation was under control.

"I'll cover the front parking lot," Jack, the custodian, informed them as he headed out of the office.

"Eleanor, where are you?" Jack searched for the assistant principal over his walkie-talkie.

"I'm headed to the north hallway," Eleanor said, knowing that would be the place students would most likely try to exit since their windows faced the incident. "I'll make sure the kids stay in their classrooms," she continued.

"What's going on?" asked Carol as she emerged from her counseling office with a student. Inquisitively, Carol pulled Theresa, a parent volunteer, aside.

Theresa said, "Johnny Castillo has been jumped by some kids from another school."

After hearing what was happening, Carol told the student she was with to wait in her office until she came back.

"Theresa, I'm heading out there," Carol said as she grabbed her keys and closed her door.

Arriving on the scene shortly after the ambulance, Carol saw Dr. Atkinson get up from Johnny's side as the paramedics began their work. Julie was across the street with Cindy as she was questioned by the police. Seeing Johnny's mother running across the street, Carol met her midstride and directed her to the side of Johnny's car a short distance from the paramedics. She looked across the street to see students staring out the windows watching the activity.

People from the neighboring homes watched from their front yards. Mothers from down the block stood with their babies in strollers to see what was happening but kept their distance.

With things calm in the front parking lot, Jack joined Dr. Atkinson, Carol, and Johnny's mother. Knowing he couldn't do anything about the neighbors, Jack told the principal, "Dr. Atkinson, I'll go and see how the kids are doing in the classes since everything is under control out here."

The ambulance took Johnny to the hospital, and Dr. Atkinson and Johnny's mother followed. Carol walked with Julie and Cindy back into the school. After writing a pass back to class for the student still in her office, Carol invited Cindy into her office to talk.

□ □ □

What a difference having a crisis plan in place makes! In both situations, even though emotions were running high, trauma was kept to a minimum. There was a plan in place that left less room for speculation and chaos. Team members moved quickly into their roles, which helped things proceed more efficiently before medical help arrived. The key to effective crisis response is for everyone to do his or her job. It takes thorough planning for all team members to know their jobs. So what are the duties of the crisis team members in an effective plan?

Roles of the Crisis Team Members

The responsibilities of the crisis team members are related to their positions on the staff. Even with the differences in emergency scenarios occurring in youth groups and Christian schools, there are many similarities between the two. We have created titles that can be used for youth group and school crisis teams: team manager, communications representative, staff representative, care-and-concern representative, facilities representative, and clerical representative. We have also included a couple of auxiliary roles you should consider: parent representative and student representative. Distinctions between youth groups and schools will be explained before going on to the next role.

The information that follows is for crises in which there is time to activate a planned response. It's not for on-the-spot emergencies where everyone fills in wherever possible as in the previous examples in this chapter.

The first position is the most intense position and carries the greatest responsibilities. This is the point person, who is the key leader on the team: the youth director or principal. We'll call this person the team manager.

Team Manager

Upon notification of an emergency, the team manager gathers as much information as possible in order to conduct an appropriate crisis response. The team manager works in conjunction with law enforcement and medical authorities in assessing the situation and needs, then consults with key ad-

visors—those in leadership positions above his or her level—
and alerts them of the crisis at hand. Youth directors would
contact church leaders or elders, and principals would get in
touch with the superintendent, board members, other administrators, and so on. These contacts would have to be determined by the church or school hierarchies.

The team manager is also responsible for conducting
meetings of various kinds. When the organization is in crisis, a crisis team meeting followed by a staff meeting should
be held at the beginning of each workday to discuss the plan
for the day and resources available. A debriefing with the crisis team at the end of the day is also important in processing
the day's events and evaluating the effectiveness of the crisis
response. In the debriefing, decisions can also be made for
any extra resources needed the following day. Contacts then
are made to procure those resources.

One of the most crucial jobs of the team manager is communication. Keeping the lines of communication open between law enforcement and medical personnel (if applicable),
crisis team members, staff and faculty, parents, and community members is essential. This can be done via walkie-
talkies or other mobile devices, phone, e-mail, meetings, and
so on. The communications representative on the crisis team
holds an important position and will work closely with the
team manager throughout this process. More of the communications rep's responsibilities will be covered shortly.

Since the team manager will be very busy dealing with all
facets of the emergency, it's the other crisis team members'

responsibility to keep the team manager updated on anything he or she should be aware of through whatever means of communication is appropriate. Different methods may be determined for different team members, making it imperative that each team member initiates updates to the team manager. It may be most reasonable to have a whiteboard or clipboard somewhere in the office out of public view but where team members can make notes of issues needing to be discussed at the next crisis team meeting.

Because the team manager is the point person, he or she is ultimately responsible for how the crisis is handled and the impact on all parties involved. A backup person must be designated to cover in the team manager's absence. This is typically the leader who is second in command after the youth director or principal. If this is the communications rep, then that person's backup will cover his or her responsibilities.

Communications Representative

The communications representative has many leadership responsibilities because of his or her leadership position in the church or school. Probably the biggest role of the communications rep is to gather and disseminate information. Dispelling rumors is crucial in the crisis response efforts. This person helps create the script the secretaries will use when dealing with the public via phone or e-mail. He or she helps the team manager with planning the crisis team meetings and the staff meetings. He or she oversees all communication efforts to and on behalf of the students, staff, parents, and community throughout the entire crisis.

One of the major responsibilities of this position is to serve as liaison with the media. This person should be aware of all church or school policies regarding communication with the media. If the church is part of a denomination or the school is part of a network of schools, there's often an employee designated to handle media issues. This must be established at the outset while developing the crisis plan and must be stated somewhere in the plan. It's in the best interest of the church or school to keep the relationship with the media as positive as possible.

If media representatives appear on the scene, it's the communications rep's responsibility to deal with them. Whatever decisions are made regarding the media, the students and staff should be informed if at all possible. Often media outlets can be forceful and report incorrect information. That's why it's important to have only one designated person handling the media.

Many churches and schools have a policy to keep the media off their grounds. If this is the case, you must let them know your policy, and then they must comply. As a result, media often set up a camera directly across the street. Let students know they may be approached by members of the media and remind them that their comments may be taken out of context. This warning may send some students heading straight for the media van, but a warning must be given anyway.

Care-and-Concern Representatives

Care-and-concern representatives are primarily advocates for youth and their families. In the youth group, the two care-and-concern reps are typically youth workers. These continually evaluate the needs of the students and try to access resources to meet their needs. Care-and-concern reps arrange informal get-togethers for the youth group so the kids can just hang out together. For the kids, these reps can facilitate prayer times and opportunities to share and process a crisis through small-group discussions or one-on-one talks.

Another important role of the care-and-concern reps is to lead a dialogue on welcoming back youth group members most deeply impacted by a crisis—victims, siblings, and so on. Often adolescents don't know what to say to these kids, so they don't say anything or avoid them all together. These reps are vital in helping with the enfolding process as these young people are integrated back into the group and in addressing rumors or misunderstandings.

In the schools, these reps are typically counselors or mental health workers in the school. If there are no such positions in your school, the school nurse or others who are known for their caring personalities will be the most appropriate persons to have in this position. These people are often easy to spot—they are always helping or reaching out to those in need.

When the team manager is initially notified of the crisis, these reps help determine the resources that will be needed. They usually will know which students will be most deeply impacted by the emergency. The care-and-concern reps can give valuable advice to the communications rep in the wording of messages sent out. They are also key in accessing appropriate outside resources to help with the response.

In the case of a death, a care-and-concern rep should be present in the deceased student's classes the first day the classes are notified. Another person is also needed in the class—usually the deceased student's counselor—to help facilitate discussion about the crisis and how the students are dealing with it. With two people in the room, if students need individual attention, there will be someone available to help those kids. On this type of day it's important to have this opportunity in class instead of just trying to get on with the scheduled lesson. Once the discussion of the crisis is finished, at least one of the reps should be available in the back of the class or in the hall to help other students who need counseling.

The care-and-concern reps can also be crucial in assisting the team manager with the difficult task of keeping in touch with the families of the victims or deceased. These reps can offer comfort and support to the family and information about resources to help them through this time. If the victim or victims are not deceased, then the care-and-concern reps can help prepare staff and students for their return.

Staff Representatives

Staff representatives serve mainly as advocates for the staff of the youth group or school. Staff reps on the youth group crisis team will represent the staff workers with the youth group. They have a crucial role in monitoring what the staff needs to perform their duties. During the initial crisis stage, they give direction to other staff members about their responsibilities. These reps are the most important links in seeing which staff members need help during and after the crisis response efforts. Their main role is to support the staff and advocate for their needs. The team manager will rely heavily on the input from the reps in designing the staff meetings to address the issues relevant to the entire staff. These reps also need to be able to quickly get input from the staff about which students need assistance.

In the schools, the staff reps should be teachers. It may be necessary to hire substitute teachers to cover staff reps' classes the first day or two of a crisis to free them up to work with impacted staff members. As with the youth groups, the team manager will depend heavily on them for input on what the staff needs in order to most effectively help the students.

Clerical Representative

The clerical representative is responsible for office management of secretaries and other office personnel during a crisis. He or she is in charge of maintaining order in the office as much as possible and will train secretaries on emergency protocol, giving them a script to use when fielding questions from the public via the phone, e-mail, etc. The clerical rep copies all forms, memos, and letters needed for the crisis response and oversees the appropriate steps in handling the records of deceased students. He or she will also help write thank-you notes to those who provide assistance during a crisis. He or she will be in charge of all documentation of the crisis and storage of the records.

Facilities Representative

The facilities representative may be on the custodial staff at the church or school, and the role is similar for both. During a crisis, this person attends to building exits, chemical storage, gas/electrical/water shutoffs, roof access to the building, and any issues related to the building. He or she is also responsible for seeing that exits are clear and that the grounds are kept safe and for increasing security checks throughout the facilities. Any cleanup of the building after a crisis will be supervised by the facilities rep, and help can be requested from appropriate parties. He or she also will train a designated backup person to perform this role on the crisis team and must inform crisis team members of building issues they need to know.

Parent Representatives

As mentioned in the first chapter, parent representatives are valuable on a youth group or school crisis team in an auxiliary role too. They can help organize parent meetings or outreach to families impacted by crises. They can also help provide other resources through their contacts or networking abilities. The duties of parent reps can be as varied as the needs in a crisis and should be determined by the crisis team.

Student Representatives

In their auxiliary roles on the crisis team, students can fill some important roles. They can serve as liaisons between students and the team manager or care-and-concern reps. These reps can be trained for specific duties on trips, as was described in the van accident example at the beginning of this chapter—getting the first-aid kit, flagging down emergency response vehicles, calling 911, and so on. They can also be trained in the skills needed to reach out to friends in crisis.

Members of the crisis team serve a vital role. As team members perform their responsibilities, each aspect of the crisis should be covered. We will delve into a more thorough discussion of each member's specific duties when we cover the immediate, short-term, and long-term phases of the crisis plan. In order for team members to perform their roles effectively, they need adequate and appropriate resources. We will discuss resources in the next chapter.

3   RESOURCES NEEDED FOR A CRISIS PLAN

With crisis team criteria established and a decision made as to which crisis possibilities will be addressed and what the responsibilities of each crisis team member will be, let's examine the resources needed to make the plan work. The most important tool for the team is the crisis team manual. Your manual will be a document that will be continually updated after every crisis because of the lessons learned.

For the last few years, as crises have unfolded in schools nationwide, I made notes and gathered information. Then, one summer, I organized and compiled the information into an easy-to-follow format. The result is this book, which I hope will guide you in getting a good start on gathering information you need for your own crisis team manual. In determining resources needed for your crisis team, the manual is the most crucial.

Crisis Team Manual

The crisis team manual is the guide that will carry you through a crisis. The crisis team won't have time to look up phone numbers online or in a phonebook or go through a stack of emergency reference books or manuals. Crisis team members need the information at their fingertips so they can move quickly through each stage of the response with confidence and ease. In chapter 12 you will find a checklist of pages I consider necessary for your crisis team manual as well as samples of many of the forms described in this chapter. The crisis team manual can be separated into five sections:

1. Contact Information
2. Emergency Response
3. Planned Response
4. Procedures/Communication
5. Forms/Documentation

Contact Information Section

The data contained in the contact information section is very important in a time of crisis. When the team manager receives word of a crisis, he or she reaches for the manual to contact the persons who will put the crisis response into motion. The first page of this section is "Crisis Contact Information." It lists the names of crisis team members along with their work, home, and cell phone numbers.

Designated sites for the "command center" follow the member information. One centralized location from which to coordinate the response efforts will be designated. The command center (often the team manager's office) will be the hub of activity and must have phone and computer access. This is where the team manager remains and law enforcement and emergency officials base their operations. The crisis team members report here as often as needed to give and receive updates. An alternate location should be designated in case the original command center location becomes unavailable. Also, an alternate location outside the building must be designated to serve as the command center in the case of evacuation.

Next on the "Crisis Contact Information" page is a list of others involved with the church or school who need to be notified of a crisis. That would include church/school leaders, board members, and so on. Next are numbers for local and community agencies that may be needed for the emergency response, such as police; fire departments; poison control centers; water, gas, and electric companies; mental health agencies; and so on.

The next page gives phone numbers within the church or school building for contacting staff or departments to inform them of the crisis. This is followed by a complete roster of work phone numbers of all staff members. After this is a listing of staff members' home phone numbers set up in a phone tree format to facilitate a quick calling system to get in touch with these persons after regular working hours. Also included will be phone numbers for off-campus staff members who do not work in the church/school building.

If feasible, a roster of students and their home contact information should be included in the manual. If you have a large youth group or school, you may depend on the information on this roster and keep it updated and stored in the Crisis Response Kit described later. The next page will be a list of phone numbers for feeder or area schools and churches. A page should be included with information on businesses and community entities that may need to know about the crisis or that you may need to contact about an emergency at their location that impacts your church or school, such as numbers of local shopping malls, businesses, and so on.

Emergency Response Section

When an emergency occurs, there may not be time to pull out your crisis team manual to look at this section. That is why this section should be reviewed again and again with the crisis team. Familiarity with the emergency response section will allow the members to move quickly into their roles without having to stop and look up what needs to be done. This section includes a checklist of emergency duties that can be reviewed and assigned at the beginning of each year so members know exactly what to do. You will also list in this section the names of staff members who are trained in CPR or first aid.

It will take time to prepare the guidelines of procedures to follow for various emergencies. We will discuss emergencies such as accidents near the church/school, fires, lockdowns, and evacuations. We will not cover emergency situations that are specific to certain geographical areas or unique activities such as drownings, hiking accidents, tornadoes, hurricanes, blizzards or snowstorms, floods or flash floods, tidal waves, lightning, thunderstorms, hazardous materials spills, violent intruders, and so on. Please consult your local experts or authorities to find out what steps your crisis team must take to prepare for these kinds of situations, and include the information in this section of the crisis team manual.

The following is a sample of information on strategies you can use in your planning, but you will adapt it to your specific group or school.

Accident on or near school/church premises. These are the duties of crisis team members:

Team manager: Assess the situation, and order the call to 911. Administer first aid or CPR if necessary. Ensure the safety of all involved. Oversee the entire response.

Communications rep: Call 911. Help manage witnesses and bystanders.

Facilities rep: Help control traffic in the area until the police arrive. Address building issues related to the accident if applicable.

Care-and-concern reps: Help console traumatized students, staff, or parents.

Clerical rep: Control the front office activity to prevent panic. Call the parents of students involved if the parents are not on scene. Document the incident on the Incident Report Form (see chapter 12).

Staff reps: Help notify all staff members of the incident—verbally for youth groups or by memo or e-mail for schools. Monitor staff needs.

After the accident is cleared and all is settled, crisis team members will meet to evaluate the response and make recommendations for next time.

In this situation, notification to student reps and parent reps who are not at the scene can be made when feasible or applicable.

Fire. If a fire occurs on the premises, immediately evacuate the staff and students following the evacuation guidelines. An evacuation map for all areas of the building should be included in the crisis manual. All crisis team members should know the designated areas to evacuate to and should have assigned areas to sweep through in the building (if possible) to make sure (1) all staff and young people are out, (2) areas of the building are cleared, and (3) doors are closed with the lights turned off. Check with your local fire department as to whether it is preferred to leave the lights on. Following are the other duties of crisis team members when a fire occurs:

Team manager: When the fire alarm sounds, the team manager will order the **communications rep** or the closest available person to make the 911 call.

The **communications rep** and the **facilities rep** will grab the Crisis Response Kits.

All crisis team members will pick up their copies of the crisis team manual on their way out of the building. Once they reach their designated location outside the building, members collect Attendance Record Sheets from staff members, accounting for all youth and staff.

If the fire is such that students have to be released to go home, documentation will be indicated on the emergency attendance sheet. Later, all members will meet to review the crisis response.

Lockdowns. Lockdowns occur when a situation outside or inside the building makes it unsafe for the students and staff. When the crisis is outside the building, typically all windows and window blinds should be closed, lights should be turned off, and everyone should get as far away from the windows as possible. (Check with your local law enforcement officials for any alterations to these instructions.) In the case of a situation inside the building, part of the structure may be put on a lockdown while the rest of the building could be ordered to evacuate. This determination will be made by law enforcement authorities. In the case of a lockdown/evacuation, staff members will follow the appropriate strategy for their particular part of the building. In case of a lockdown, these are the other duties of crisis team members:

Team manager: When the team manager is notified of the lockdown, he or she will make an announcement by the most appropriate method determined in previous discussions by the crisis team. In schools, this is usually over the intercom system. Here's a sample announcement: "May I have your attention, please? May I have your attention, please? We need to secure the building. We need to secure the building. Lock down your room. Lock down your room. This is a lockdown situation inside {outside} the building. This is a lockdown situation inside [outside] the building." That's all that is needed for the announcement. Teachers will know they need to act immediately. The team manager then follows the directions of the authorities as to his or her responsibilities during the lockdown. He or she conveys further instructions to crisis team members as directed.

All crisis team members: All members must remain in lockdown in their areas unless otherwise instructed by the team manager. Crisis team members may be needed to sweep through the building or may have to stay in their designated areas. The team manager will make that determination with the help of the law enforcement officials on the scene.

Later, all members meet to review the crisis response.

Evacuation. An evacuation occurs when a situation inside the building calls for everyone to get out. Typically, there will be designated areas for everyone to report to that are farther away from the building than the distance used during a fire drill. Ideally, there will be another building within walking distance where everyone can go. In case of an evacuation, these are the duties of crisis team members:

Team manager: Upon receiving word from authorities for the need to evacuate, the team manager will make the announcement to evacuate by the appropriate method. Here's a sample announcement: "May I have your attention, please? May I have your attention, please? We need to

evacuate the building. We need to evacuate the building."
If an area of the school needs to be avoided because of the
emergency situation, then the team manager will add
"Avoid the _____ [location]. Avoid the
_____ [location]." That's all that's needed
for the announcement. Teachers will know they need to act
immediately. The team manager then follows the directions of the authorities as to his or her responsibilities during the evacuation and will convey further instructions to
crisis team members as directed.

Communications rep and **facilities rep:** Pick up the
Crisis Response Kits and go to the evacuation site.

All crisis team members: Each member should pick up
his or her crisis team manual and sweep through the area
of the building he or she is assigned to check (if applicable). Once at the evacuation area, team members will collect the Attendance Record Sheets from staff members.

If the evacuation is such that the students can be released
to their parents, that will be indicated on the Attendance
Record Sheet.

Later, all members meet to review the crisis response.

Planning for the situations listed in this section is difficult, because they happen without warning. However, discussions and preparation beforehand can prevent possibly fatal mistakes. The emergencies we have addressed and those
listed at the beginning of this section that have not been addressed should be covered in the crisis manual. You may nev-

er face some of these situations, but it's better to be ready in case they do arise.

Planned Response Section

Youth groups and schools experience situations that allow for a strategic response, meaning the crisis team has time to meet to plan and coordinate its response. When the crisis team initially meets, an Incident Report form can help the team sort through the facts of the crisis to determine what steps need to be taken. A Students/Staff Impacted by the Incident form will help determine who may need extra support. This can be followed by filling out the Determining the Expected Degree of Trauma form that can be used to help the crisis team estimate how much the church or school may be affected and what outside resources may be needed.

This section must also include Crisis Team Member Responsibilities pages to delineate the responsibilities of crisis team members during each phase of the crisis response. This is easiest to follow when it is listed in a step-by-step process. Then, as the crisis unfolds, there's less room for error, because everyone knows his or her responsibilities and will be more prepared for unexpected surprises. This will allow for an orderly response in the midst of sometimes chaotic circumstances. At various times during the crisis response, team members can refer to the crisis team manual to make sure they are covering all areas of the plan. Most of the information that goes in this section will be detailed in chapters four, seven, and nine of this book. You can refer to those chapters when preparing this part of your manual.

Procedures/Communication Section

In this section, list procedures and protocol for various parts of the crisis response plan. The first form in this section is the Staff Responsibilities form to help staff members know what's expected of them in a time of crisis. Next, it's important to include various maps of the church or school building to help people know the layout of the building, evacuation routes, fire drill exit routes, and the locations of the gas, water, and electrical shutoffs. Information regarding schedules and activities is helpful to include in this section.

This section should have samples that the crisis team can refer to when creating various communications that may need to go out. This is where you can have information on developing memos to be read in classes or meetings and parent letters to be sent home. You can include sample scripts for secretaries to use while answering phone inquiries about the crisis. The form Strategies for Dealing with the Media will help you understand important things to consider if you face an onslaught of media requests.

Public address announcements during lockdowns or evacuations can be addressed here to include the wording of announcements over the intercom to alert the school of emergency situations such as the ones presented earlier for lockdowns and evacuations. There should be a standard format for announcements so the staff will know exactly what's happening. You also need to state in the crisis manual which staff members will make the announcements. Typically the team manager will be the one to make announcements on the intercom, but there should be people designated for backup in case the team manager is unavailable.

Forms/Documentation Section

Documentation of all aspects of the crisis is vital. The most important form in this section is the Attendance Record Sheet. Taking attendance is not usually considered necessary for youth groups, as it is for schools, but during a crisis you'll need to know the locations of all students. The process for the release of students to parents also should be covered in this section. Careful records must be kept regarding students present and those who may have disappeared during an incident. These records can help locate missing students or determining if any students played a part in the case of false alarms.

The Students Counseled form can be used to log the names of students who are seen by staff, counselors, leaders, or administrators, and so on to talk about the crisis. This helps the staff keep track of who's getting help and those you may need to keep an eye on. It is also useful, in the school setting, to keep track of students who may be using the crisis to get out of class. Names of students from these lists can be compiled on a form called Impacted Students to be distributed to staff members so they can see which kids may need extra support. The care-and-concern reps will take the list to plan the follow-up for those students.

One final form in this section is the Emergency Personnel Check-in Sheet. This is important in documenting information on people other than emergency services personnel who come from outside your church or school to help. If you have people volunteering, this will enable you to have record of their presence to verify who they are and their credentials to help. It's important to have this list in areas most accessible to the public to ensure they sign in when they arrive. Even if you know the volunteers, they should sign the form in case the need arises later to follow up on a problem situation.

Front Pocket of the Manual

In the front pocket of the crisis team manual you can place items that need to be readily available. First, put in about 10 copies of the Attendance Record Sheet discussed earlier. Another important piece is a red/green card—two cards that are laminated together so that one side shows red and the other shows green.

If a lockdown occurs, the red/green card is used to indicate if there's trouble in a room. If the room has a window, the card is placed in the window. If the red side is showing, that indicates help is needed—someone is wounded, someone is missing, or so on. If the green side is showing, then everything is OK. This allows emergency personnel to move quickly through a building as they assess the situation. If rooms don't have a window, you may not be able to use this method because if the cards are placed outside the room—on a clip on the door, for example—they could be turned by an intruder, causing the additional problem of emergency personnel having incorrect information. The crisis team should discuss whether this is feasible for your building or if there are alternative options.

It's an ongoing process to develop a crisis team manual. The addition, deletion, or changes in the material is an ongoing process. However, it can save lives, so it's very important to keep the information current with regular revisions.

This covers the main parts of the crisis team manual. A checklist of these forms and some samples are located in chapter 12. You may think of other items you want to include in your crisis plan. Besides the manual there are other important resources you'll need.

Staff Emergency Folder

A school in our district uses separate folders for all the staff with crisis information and procedures, so we incorporated the idea into our plan. Since not all of our staff members have a crisis team manual, we include information in the folder that all staff members need to know when crises arise. The folders are a unique color—not our school colors or a typical color used by everyone—so it stands out and is easy to spot. The folders have prongs and front and back pockets. Teachers are instructed to keep the folder by their grade books or in a visible place on their desks. Staff members know to grab their staff emergency folder along with their grade books when a fire drill sounds or an emergency occurs.

Pages from the crisis team manual that are relevant to what the staff needs to know are included in the folder. They don't need all the information the crisis team has, so these folders have significantly fewer pages than the crisis team manual. We have received positive comments from staff about the folders because it allows the staff members to feel some control when crises hit because they have all the information within reach. The crisis team can determine which pages from the crisis team manual would be appropriate for the staff emergency folder.

Crisis Team Phone Cards

It's important for all crisis team members to have the contact information for other team members available to them at all times. Since the crisis team manual may not always be accessible, we created a card to put in our wallets or purses. On the card we list the team members' names and their home, work, and cell phone numbers (see chapter 12).

Crisis Team Badges

Each crisis team member should be provided with an identification badge to be kept with his or her crisis team manual. The badges should display the name of the person's church or school and identify him or her as a crisis team member. These badges will alert emergency personnel as to who is qualified and trained to help. This should prevent situations in which imposters could get in and cause problems or become privy to confidential information. The badge should be worn in all crisis situations.

Having the right resources makes your crisis response effort more effective with less chance for error. It takes a lot of time to complete the requirements listed in this section. But your efforts will be rewarded at the intervention stage when you likely won't have time to collaborate with others. The more familiar your crisis team becomes with the plan and these resources, the less time it will take to implement the plan when the time comes.

Youth groups and Christian schools have different needs in the midst of a crisis. In the prevention stage of a crisis plan, the crisis team tries to anticipate and prepare for all that can happen when tragedy strikes. The plan continues to evolve and improve with each crisis, and adaptations of prevention strategies will help in an emergency. In the intervention stage, the members must be ready to act without notice. If the prevention planning is adequate, the intervention stage will run more smoothly. It is impossible to plan for everything that may happen during the intervention stage, but good prevention planning can give you confidence that as many areas are covered as possible.

The first two days following a crisis are the most crucial. Leadership performance during these two days will affect for a long time to come the impact the crisis has on those involved.

Each leadership position is listed separately along with its corresponding duties. It is suggested that you use this layout to present this material in your crisis team manual, because it will allow team members to be concerned with only the pages that apply to their specific responsibilities. This Crisis Team Member Representatives form presents a checklist format that can be adapted for your crisis team manual.

Because crisis responses will not be the same for youth groups as it is for schools, we will note next to each entry whether the task is just for youth groups (Y), schools (S), or both (Y/S).

After selecting the tasks that are relevant to your youth group or school, put everything into the format of the Crisis Team Member Representatives section. This is the format we have found most efficient and useful in a crisis situation.

Throughout the chapter, we'll list titles of forms to use for different purposes. These forms were explained in chapter 3, and samples are shown in chapter 12.

Team Manager Responsibilities

- After initially receiving the information, contact designated church/school leaders (senior pastor, elders, superintendent, administrators, board members, etc.), law enforcement and medical personnel, or other related first response officials. (Y/S)

- When appropriate, contact parents/guardians of the victim/deceased as soon as possible. Arrange for a time to stop by to visit the family. Ask permission to give out information to the students. (Y/S)

- Verify all facts before releasing any information (people involved, location, description of incident, cause, time and date of occurrence). Consider confidentiality issues. Contact local victim assistance agencies if there is a need for information or guidance. (Y/S)

- Contact crisis team members and set a time for a crisis team meeting and staff meeting. (Y/S)

- Contact all youth group leaders about the crisis. Also take into consideration other leaders in the church who may have contact with the student, such as Sunday School teachers, nursery workers, or others who may supervise the student in volunteer work. (Y)

- Determine a strategy to notify youth group members via a phone tree, or in case there is a nonyouth activity at the church in progress, have an announcement made about a brief youth group meeting immediately following the activity. Consideration should also be given to staff and students who are absent when the information is released. (Y)

- Determine strategies to notify staff and students via memo, staff meeting, phone tree, and so on. Remember that staff includes cafeteria workers, custodians, aides, coaches, and so on. Consideration should also be given to staff and students who are absent when the information is released. (S)

- In the case of a death, before the phone tree is activated, make a personal call to teachers of the student, both current and past teachers, or other staff members who knew the student well. (S)

- If the phone tree is to be activated for staff members, first record the phone message on the church/school voice mail system. (Y/S)

- Instruct the communications rep to activate the staff phone tree with instructions for staff to check their voice mail for details about the crisis. (Y/S)

- Get packets for initial crisis team meeting from the clerical rep. (Incident Report Form, Students/Staff Impacted by the Incident, and the Crisis Team Member Responsibilities) (Y/S)

- Facilitate crisis team meetings. (Y/S)

- Help identify staff members who may need extra support, and arrange for follow-up contacts with them periodically. (Students/Staff Impacted by the Incident) (Y/S)

- Help identify students who may be particularly affected by this crisis. (Students/Staff Impacted by the Incident) (Y/S)

- Assign to the communications rep the continuing task of gathering and disseminating information about the crisis. (Y/S)

- Help dispel rumors. (Y/S)

- Make decisions with input from the appropriate church leaders and the communications rep regarding the media. (Y)

- Make decisions with input from the appropriate school leaders and the communications rep regarding the media. (S)

- Arrange for substitute teachers as needed. (S)

- Arrange for the staff meeting. (Y/S)

  When _____

  Where _____

  Who will facilitate _____

- Facilitate the staff meeting. (Y/S)

- Instruct staff members to refer all information and questions to the team manager or communications rep. (Y/S)

- If applicable, get staff volunteers to make hospital visits. (Y/S)

- Assign the care-and-concern reps to help organize food outreaches to the family of the victim/deceased. (Y)

- Contact the parent reps to help organize food outreaches to the family of the victim/deceased. (S)
- If needed, assign the clerical rep to arrange for extra clerical help. (Y/S)
- Work with the communications rep and clerical rep to determine procedures to release information. If appropriate, work with the communications rep to develop a written statement to use when receiving calls. If appropriate, include hospital, medical facility, or funeral information as it's available. (Y/S)
- If there's a death, give authorization for the clerical rep to remove the name of the deceased from all related lists. (Y/S)
- If necessary, coordinate with the communications rep and care-and-concern reps to prepare a letter to send home. (Y/S)
- Facilitate daily crisis team meetings for reviews and planning for the next day. (Y/S)
- Facilitate staff meetings as necessary to review or discuss the crisis. (Y/S)
- If appropriate, give input to the family of the deceased about funeral/memorial service suggestions. (See chapter 8.) (Y/S)

Communications Rep Responsibilities

- After receiving word about the crisis from the team manager, work with him or her to verify details of the crisis, and set the time for the crisis team meeting and staff meeting. (Y/S)

- Discuss with the team manager the best strategy to notify the staff and students. (Y/S)

- If the phone tree needs to be activated, make the calls under designated responsibilities. (Y/S)

- Help the team manager with facilitation of the crisis team meeting as designated by the team manager. (Y/S)

- Continue to gather and disseminate information as received. (Y/S)

- Help dispel rumors. (Y/S)

- Make decisions with the team manager regarding the media, and inform staff and students regarding media decisions. (Y/S)

- Help make the necessary contacts to arrange for substitute teacher coverage. (S)

- Help the team manager with the staff meeting. (Y/S)

- Help identify staff members who may need extra support. (Students/Staff Impacted by the Incident). (Y/S)

- Help identify students who may be particularly affected by this crisis. (Students/Staff Impacted by the Incident). (Y/S)

- Work with the care and concern reps and staff reps to write a memo for teachers to read to their classes about the crisis and where to go for support. (Sample Memo to Classes) (S)

- Work with the team manager and clerical rep to determine procedures to release information. If appropriate, work with the team manager to develop a written statement to use for secretaries receiving calls, and include

hospital, medical facility, or funeral information as it's available. (Y/S)

- Help dispel rumors. (Y/S)
- If necessary, prepare with the team manager and care-and-concern reps a letter to parents to send home. (Y/S)
- Attempt to contact and inform absent staff members. (Y/S)
- Assist the team manager in facilitating daily crisis team meetings for reviews and planning for the next day. (Y/S)
- Get the list of Impacted Students from the clerical rep, and help distribute the forms to the staff. (Y/S)
- Follow up as needed with leaders/officials, church/school leaders, elders, board members, and so on. (Y/S)
- Pursue extra resources deemed necessary. (Y/S)

Care-and-Concern Rep Responsibilities

- Coordinate with the team manager for a time to visit the home of the victim's or deceased student's family. (Y/S)
- If applicable, designate a point person for ongoing communication with outside mental health support agencies. (Y/S)
- Help the team manager identify resources needed for the crisis. (Y/S)
- If requested, give input to the team manager about the announcement via voice mail and the phone tree alerting the staff to check their voice mail. (Y/S)

- Discuss with the team manager the staff members who need to be contacted personally by him or her before the phone tree is activated. (Y/S)

- Attend the crisis team meeting and give input or background information on the students or staff involved in the crisis. (Y/S)

- If requested, help the team manager plan the staff meeting. (Y/S)

- Help identify staff members who may need extra support, and follow up with them periodically. (Students/ Staff Impacted by the Incident) (Y/S)

- Help identify students who may be particularly affected by this crisis. (Students/Staff Impacted by the Incident) (Y/S)

- Help dispel rumors. (Y/S)

- Distribute Students Counseled to all counselors, leaders, and others who will work with struggling students. (Y/S)

- Designate a counselor and support person to follow the victim's schedule—to process the incident with the classes and offer support to students individually and/or as a group. (S)

- Establish places where students and staff can go for support: (youth leaders' offices, youth group room, counseling office, conference room, staff lounge). (Y/S)

  Room _____

  Facilitator _____

  Room _____

Facilitator _____

Room _____

Facilitator _____

- Work with the team manager to get staff volunteers to make hospital visits. (Y/S)

- Coordinate with the communications rep the creation of the memo for teachers to read to classes about the crisis and where to go for support. (Sample Memo to Classes) (S)

- Assist in the distribution of the memo to the classes. Assist in reading the memo to the class if the teacher is unable to read it. Make sure the memo is read immediately and not delayed until later in the class period. (S)

- Work with parent reps to organize food outreaches to the family. (Y/S)

- Inform secretaries how/where to send students who come to the office for support. (S)

- Record on Students Counseled form all students counseled. (Y/S)

- If necessary, assist the team manager and communications rep with preparation of a letter to send home about the crisis. (Y/S)

- Collect, coordinate, and provide resources for families. (Y/S)

- Attend the daily crisis team meetings, and add input as warranted. (Y/S)

- Get the list titled Impacted Students from the clerical rep, and help distribute the forms to the staff. (Y/S)

- Arrange for leaders/counselors to call parents of highly impacted students—not all the students listed on the Impacted Students list. (Y/S)
- If the opportunity is presented, discuss funeral/memorial service recommendations with the family of the deceased. (See chapter 8.) (Y/S)
- When applicable, help coordinate classroom remembrance and "empty chair" activities for classes of the deceased student. (See chapter 8.) (S)
- If the topic of establishing a memorial in honor of the deceased arises, discuss the issue as needed. (See chapter 8.) (Y/S)

Staff Rep Responsibilities

- After he or she has received word of the crisis, help the team manager determine which staff members need a personal contact prior to the phone tree being activated. (Y/S)
- Attend the crisis team meeting, and give input on staff concerns/issues. (Y/S)
- Help identify staff members who may need extra support, and follow up with them periodically. (Students/ Staff Impacted by the Incident) (Y/S)
- Help identify students who may be particularly affected by this crisis. (Students/Staff Impacted by the Incident) (Y/S)
- Help the team manager plan the staff meeting. (Y/S)
- Help the communications rep write the memo the

teachers read to classes about the crisis and where to go for support. (Sample Memo to Classes) (S)

- Distribute the memo to classrooms, and assist in reading the memo to the class if the teacher is unable to read it. Make sure the memo is read immediately and not delayed until later in the class period. (S)
- Help dispel rumors. (Y/S)
- Check in each day with departments to see how the staff is doing. (S)
- Encourage staff members to keep an eye on each other and reach out to struggling staff members, or let the staff reps or care-and-concern reps know. (Y/S)
- Be available for questions and concerns from staff. (Y/S)
- Coordinate with the care-and-concern reps and outside resources for ongoing staff support. (Y/S)
- Attend daily meetings with the crisis team, and offer input on staff issues. (Y/S)
- Help the team manager plan crisis-related staff meetings. (Y/S)

Clerical Rep Responsibilities

- After receiving word about the crisis, prepare the room for the crisis team meeting. (Y/S)
- Make sure packets of pages from the crisis team manual —Incident Report Form, Students/Staff Impacted by the Incident, Crisis Team Member Responsibilities— are ready for all members for the initial crisis team meeting. Take notes at the crisis team meeting. (Y/S)
- Reserve the room for the staff meeting. (Y/S)

- Help identify staff members who may need extra support. (Students/Staff Impacted by the Incident) (Y/S)
- Help identify students who may be particularly affected by this crisis. (Students/Staff Impacted by the Incident) (Y/S)
- If needed, arrange for extra clerical help. (Y/S)
- Help dispel rumors. (Y/S)
- Work with the team manager and communications rep to determine procedures to release information. If appropriate, work with the communications rep to develop a written statement for secretaries to use when receiving calls, and include hospital, medical facility, or funeral information as it is available. (Y/S)
- Let receptionists/secretaries know of procedures to release information. (Y/S)
- Tell secretaries to refer all media calls to the communications rep. (Y/S)
- Type and copy the memo to be read in classrooms. (S)
- If applicable, type and copy the parent letter to be sent home with the students regarding the crisis. (S)
- If there is the death of a student—
    remove the name from absentee list. (S)
    remove the name from mailing lists. (Y/S)
    delete schedule off central computer to avoid automatic dialer absentee calls. (S)
    retrieve any correspondence in progress. (Y/S)
    send a note to collect personal belongings and class projects from teachers. (S)
    clear all fines. (S)

- Create a form called Impacted Students, and on it type all students' names listed on the Students Counseling forms and the Students/Staff Impacted by the Incident forms. Make copies for all staff members with a cover sheet stating that the list is confidential. Give the forms to the communications rep, care-and-concern reps, or staff reps for distribution. (Y/S)
- Take notes at all crisis team meetings and staff meetings, and file documentation in appropriate places. (Y/S)

Facilities Rep Responsibilities

- Upon receiving initial word of the crisis, determine whether or not to lock certain doors and/or shut off some or all utilities.
- Help emergency personnel as requested. (Y/S)
- If applicable, close off or limit access to affected areas of the building involved in the crisis. (Y/S)
- Increase security checks. (Y/S)
- Attend the initial crisis team meeting. (Y/S)
- Help dispel rumors. (Y/S)
- Help identify staff members who may need extra support. (Students/Staff Impacted by the Incident) (Y/S)
- Help identify students who may be particularly affected by this crisis. (Students/Staff Who May Be Impacted) (Y/S)
- If there is a death, after school hours clean out the locker and change the locker combination. Give the student's belongings to the care-and-concern reps. (S)

- Contact facility managers at other schools if applicable. (S)
- Attend all crisis team meetings. (Y/S)

Parent Rep Responsibilities

- Upon receiving word of the crisis, work with the crisis team to determine support that may be needed by the family directly impacted. (Y/S)
- Help dispel rumors. (Y/S)
- Work with volunteers to organize food outreaches to the family. (Y/S)
- Work with volunteers to provide food for staff and crisis workers. (Y/S)
- Work with volunteers to provide food at the church for the youth group as it gathers. (Y)
- Provide crisis updates and needs to parents via e-mail if applicable. (Y/S)
- Keep the crisis team updated about the needs of the parent community. (Y/S)
- Help the team manager organize a parent meeting if necessary. (Y/S)
- Encourage parents to attend viewings or funerals with their kids. (Y/S)

Student Rep Responsibilities

- Be a liaison to the crisis team concerning needs of the young people. (Y/S)
- Help dispel rumors. (Y/S)

The first two days of crisis response are crucial in determining the lasting effects on a church or school. The crisis team members must be diligent in carrying out their responsibilities to minimize the detrimental impact the crisis may have on the young people.

5 TIPS ON REACHING OUT TO KIDS

Young people experience tragedy differently than adults, and they're often hindered in their process of healing because of the ways in which adults attempt to help. It's crucial for those in youth ministry to have a good understanding of an adolescent's perspective in order to know effective ways to reach out. In this chapter we'll explain what kids may experience, reasons for their behavior, and ways you can help.

Through this entire process, prayer is the most important factor. What we address in this chapter is what we've found to work in our own experiences, but these may not work in every situation. God knows just what your students need, so be in prayer continually throughout the crisis, asking for His wisdom and discernment each step of the way.

Through Their Eyes

When a crisis occurs, it's important to understand that young people view it differently than adults. Through our vast experiences as adults, we have a greater understanding of the big picture and the ramifications of the incident. Kids see the situation only in the intensity of the moment. They'll first struggle with making sense of the situation, then they'll need validation of their experience, and next they'll try to figure out how it impacts them personally.

When facing a crisis, students want information and details. They want to know as much as possible about the crisis, and they'll likely ask lots of questions. In the case of a death or crisis in which none of your students were present to know what happened, get permission from the parents of those involved to know what you can share. Ask the parents if you can mention the circumstances surrounding the incident, who was involved, and so on.

In a large youth group or school, some of the students may not recognize the names of those involved, so they may ask for photos of them. Try to use a photo from a yearbook or an activity they attended. The kids may feel the need to see a photo because then they'll be able to understand how the crisis impacts them personally.

Following an accidental death at a school in a nearby city, students went to the counselor's office regularly to see a photo of the student who died. If when they saw it they realized they didn't know the person, their faces reflected their relief. But when they recognized the person, they had various reactions. It's best for adults to have possession of the photo so that when students come to see it, the adults can monitor how the kids are doing and determine who may need extra support.

How closely the young people are connected to those involved will determine their responses. It's a given that those students who are more closely linked to the students involved in the incident will be more deeply impacted. Also, those close to the victims will typically hear of the incident sooner than others, so they'll be at a different stage of the process. There will likely be rumors surfacing, and it is important to help dispel those rumors as quickly as possible.

One interesting thing that happens among the students is the reaction of those closest to the people involved in the incident. I've heard best friends say, "Why is she crying? She didn't even know Jake." It's a sentiment that since that person wasn't really close to the victim, he or she must be faking it or just trying to fit in with insiders. It's as if it becomes a game of one-upmanship to see who knew the person better and who will be impacted the most. Counselors see that happen again and again.

Since the inner circle of those most impacted get the most attention and help, others may long to receive that attention as well. Leaders must pay attention to these situations if they begin to surface. You must address all students needing help, even those you think may be doing it to get attention. Reach out to them, but don't let them dominate your attention. In group settings as kids are sharing their grief, if one person dominates the time, try to ask questions to get others involved. You can even make the comment "Sheri, I appreciate what you have to share, but we want to make sure everyone has a chance to talk."

If that person continues, during a break (even create a restroom break if necessary), have a leader take that student off to the side to explain to him or her that everyone needs a chance to share. Tell the student that he or she can even come in to talk to you and another leader after the meeting. If the student is acting up just to get attention, he or she probably won't want to meet with you separately away from the group. If that doesn't help, then recommend professional help for the student. Often those wanting attention are dealing with loss issues of their own that the leaders may not be aware of.

If it's a case in which a student may be talking about suicide and you think it may be just to get attention, you must take their comments seriously. If the student claims to have a plan, time, and the means of committing suicide (for example, "I'm going to shoot myself with my dad's gun tomorrow when my parents leave for the weekend"), you must act on it immediately. Meet with the parents and recommend an immediate evaluation from a mental health professional at a hospital or similar place.

At times I've dealt with students who made several suicide threats. With each threat we made the necessary intervention—talking, counseling, and so on. If the student's parents and I thought he or she was probably bluffing, the parent took the student to the hospital to get an evaluation. After that grueling process, not one of those students ever made another threat. Even if the student doesn't have a plan but has made comments about taking his or her own life, you must act on it.

Look Beyond the Obvious

Sometimes when people lose a loved one, they may experience the flooding of unresolved loss issues within themselves. For example, a big, strapping football player came to me after the death of a student at the church he attended. He said he didn't know why he was crying because he didn't know the student well. I asked him if he ever felt this way before, and he immediately said he had not. Then, as he thought a little more, he realized he had.

"When I was eight my cat died," he explained. "I started crying when we were burying him, but my dad said, 'Don't cry. Big boys don't cry,' so I stopped crying."

"So you never cried anymore about the cat?" I asked.

"No," he said.

"Were there other times you felt this way?"

"Oh, yes. Two years later my parents divorced. My uncle took me fishing each weekend the next summer. At the end of that summer my uncle died." Tears began to well up in his eyes. "I began to cry at his funeral, but I remembered that since my dad was gone, I needed to be strong for my mom." Tears came rushing forth.

"So you never had the chance to cry about your uncle either?" I asked.

He shook his head. He was finally able to mourn the loss of his cat and uncle. The tears flowed for a few minutes as he honored those precious times in his life and his loved ones. His heart was so much lighter when he left the office. That's why this work is so crucial to our youth. I see many adults with unresolved losses that hinder the quality of their existence and their relationships. It's a difficult work, but God can use us to "bind up the brokenhearted, to proclaim freedom for the captives" (Isa. 61:1).

Leaders should jot down the names of those who are close to the victims who may be out of town at the time of the incident. Special effort should be made to contact them as soon as possible upon their return. Often friends may contact them while they're away, so you should check in with them to see if they need support while they're gone. They'll face unique issues when they arrive home.

In seeing the crisis through the kids' eyes, you'll be able to help them understand what they need to do to process their grief, and you can answer their questions. Figuring out ways it affects them personally will give them parameters of appropriate expectations for their healing process. They want information and modeling from the adults to know what to expect. If we can validate each student and let the student know that what he or she is experiencing is normal for his or her life experience, the student will be able to rest in knowing that he or she can follow your model of how to move through the crisis. Seeing your understanding and support for where the student is will free him or her up to not have to try to live up to the expectations of others. One exception is if there is inappropriate behavior.

Understanding Their Behavior

Besides the stress of handling the logistics of a crisis, one surprise for many youth workers is the behavior they may encounter from some kids. This area is one of the greatest challenges, because some of the things you will experience are unexpected and may catch you off guard.

A crucial part of seeing through the eyes of the kids is an understanding that every student may react differently to the news of a crisis. We must avoid conveying expectations of how the kids should be handling the situation—like the father who said big boys don't cry. When you have a big group meeting with all the kids present, it's important to discuss that people react differently to crises. Some will be sad, some mad, some in shock, and some talking incessantly. It all depends on each person's point of reference and their past experiences.

We must validate all of the young people and where they are in their process in order to be OK with their behavior. Yet if kids are being bothered by the way some are behaving, the situation should be handled carefully. Do what you can for each student so he or she will be able to process the crisis in his or her own way without hurting or impinging on someone else. Some kids will cling to their friends, and some may want to be alone. Some may want to play a game or be active, while some may just want to sit and cry and reminisce. There is some important information you will want to pass on to parents too.

Disputes often arise in families during crises, because the parents' needs are different than the kids' needs. In the tragedies I've dealth with, I noticed that parents wanted to cling to their sons and daughters and not let them out of their sight, but the kids wanted to be with their friends instead of their families.

The kids longed to be together because they had shared this experience, and they didn't have to explain anything or answer the many questions their parents and others were asking. They could relate to each other because they shared the same fears, confusion, and questions about the incident. I've seen this disconnect between parents and children in many crisis situations through the years.

Don't be surprised if the students ask tough questions. No matter what their spiritual beliefs are, most kids will have questions about why God allowed the incident to happen. If they do, let them talk through those issues, and don't tell them they shouldn't feel that way. There aren't any pat answers. Don't try to explain away something that you don't know. The most important thing is to be honest. If you don't know the answer, admit it. If they insist on an answer, then seek help at an appropriate time from a qualified professional. Be careful not to be condescending or to come across as all-knowing.

Survivor's Guilt

Survivor's guilt is a reality for a lot of young people who survived a tragedy that took the lives of others. This can present in many different ways. It can arise in those who were on the scene at the time of the incident. For example, survivors of school shootings who were right next to someone who was killed may have wondered, *Why did he get killed and not me? Is there anything I could have done to save him?* or *I should have done more to save her* or *He did more for others—he deserved to live more than me.* They may feel they didn't deserve to be spared.

Another form of survivor's guilt surfaces when a person is not present when the incident occurred at a time he or she normally would have been there. One student who would normally have been at her school, left with a friend to get lunch at a fast-food restaurant. To this day she wonders if she could have helped her friend who was stabbed by her former boyfriend.

Survivor's guilt is often detected in those who follow directions during a crisis. Students and teachers who are ordered to leave the building during a fire or some other catastrophe may feel guilty for leaving after hearing of heroic acts others performed to save lives. They may always wonder if they could have stayed to help one more person out of the building. Law enforcement personnel say it's always better to follow the instructions of the authorities than to try to stay back and rescue. Those who stay can actually hinder the efforts of law enforcement officials by hanging around after the command has been given to evacuate or leave the scene. It's always best to leave the response efforts to trained professionals.

Contradictory behavior is a typical reaction in some people. Kids may act in ways that are atypical compared to their normal behavior. If they're usually not emotional, they may become very emotional. Other examples are talkative students who become very quiet, or withdrawn people who begin to talk incessantly. These are typical reactions to crises. If it lasts for months, it's advisable to seek professional help for that young person.

Another behavior to watch for is a youngster's heightened sense of vulnerability or feelings of being unsafe. Do everything possible to ensure the safety of your students, and share details with them about the steps you've taken to keep them safe. This is also important in working with parents.

There may be some kids who will dwell on the graphic details of the tragedy. They may want to focus on the blood, gore, and horror of the scene. Allow them to talk about it if you can handle it, or ask someone else to talk with them. Pull them aside from the larger group if others are being adversely affected by that kind of talk. If they dwell on it for days, try to refocus the conversation. If it continues, you may need to recommend they see a professional counselor.

Another behavior alteration to watch for is difficulty in sleeping. Some students may have recurring nightmares of what they saw, heard, smelled, and so on. If this continues, consider counseling. Encourage the students to rest their bodies even if they can't fall asleep.

Students may experience a change in their eating habits. They may not want to eat, or they may eat continually. Provide healthful snacks for them, and encourage them to eat even if they don't feel like it. Some may indulge in comfort foods. This is not desirable long-term, but it's OK for a short time as long as no other health issues are involved. Encourage them to eat healthfully as much as possible. If poor eating or lack of eating continues, encourage them to seek help from a professional.

Tangible Ways to Help

There are effective ways to help your students reach out to each other during this time too. The students will be looking to you to model the correct response to the crisis. If you can help them find ways to reach out to each other, it will help lessen your load as you try to balance all facets of the crisis.

The best way you can help these students is to simply be present. You don't need to know all the answers—just let them know you care. Sometimes the best thing you can do is sit with them in silence. Don't tell them you know how they feel, because you don't. Each person's experience with a crisis is based on his or her own perceptions, relationship with those involved in the crisis, and experiences. Be honest with the students.

Sometimes the tendency is to avoid people who are hurting. If you don't know what to say, tell them that. Just simply saying, "I don't know what to say, but I want you to know I'm here for you," is more helpful than you know. You can also ask the person, "How can I help you? Is there something you need that I can get you or that I can do for you?" Most of the time the response will be no, but it's important that the student knows you want to do anything you can. Try never to say, "If you need anything, call me." Ninety-nine times out of a hundred, that's not interpreted as a real offer to help. This is why it's important to follow up as often as possible.

In the youth group or school setting, staff members can share the duties of following up with students who are in need of support. The Impacted Students List will help the care-and-concern reps determine who needs to follow up with each student. The staff member closest to the students will typically be responsible in a youth group. In a school, a counselor or another person will typically be assigned to each student. That's why it's important to keep the list of Impacted Students nearby so the staff will know who needs their attention.

Another way to help the young people is to explain the grieving process to them. The most expedient way to describe this process is Elisabeth Kübler-Ross's model of the five stages of grief. In her book *On Death and Dying,* she describes the five stages as—

1. Denial and isolation—this includes shock and withdrawal.

2. Anger—at the person inflicting the hurt (even if he or she is dead), anger at society, or anger at self. If not dealt with accordingly, we may displace our anger on innocent bystanders.

3. Bargaining—asking oneself, *If I {or he or she} had only done this or that, this might not have happened,* and so on.

4. Depression—a numbing feeling often coupled with anger and sadness.

5. Acceptance—when the sting of the pain subsides, reality hits, and the loss is finally acknowledged.[1]

The stages can take a different amount of time for each person. Some people don't go through all the stages, and some repeat stages. The kids will go through the stages in their own timing, so it's not necessary to try to help them get from one stage to another.

Some people who don't understand the grief process make comments such as "She should be over it by now," "He's a wimp," or "That happened years ago." Those comments can drive the pain deeper. Sometimes people get stuck in one of the first four grief stages. If one of your students seems stuck in a stage for many months, you may suggest that he or she seek help from a professional. It's also natural to revisit a stage. This often happens at the anniversaries of the loss (one month, one year, the first Christmas after, and so on).

Grief that follows trauma may seem unbearable at times, but it's actually a crucial part of the healing process. Persons who are stifled during the middle stage of the process and are unable to work through that stage may struggle with that area throughout their lives until they are finally able to work through it.

You can also reach out to young people by assisting them in finding activities that will help them process their feelings. The key is to offer different kinds of activities, because not all youth will grieve in the same way. One way is to help with the coordination of food deliveries to the impacted family or to simply drop off something to the family. For some it's important to spend time with the family; for others that will be too difficult.

Another great idea is for someone to open up his or her home as a place where the kids can just hang out together.

Early on, the grief can be intense, but eventually the kids will simply enjoy being together. They may even want to watch videos or DVDs or listen to their favorite music. There should always be adult supervision to see how the kids are doing. Here are some important tips for helping teens cope with trauma:

- Be direct, simple, honest, and appropriate. Explain truthfully what happened.

- Listen to what the teen is feeling or asking you. Then respond according to the teen's needs and your own ability.

- Encourage the teen to express feelings openly. Crying is normal and helpful. So are feelings of anger.

- Accept the emotions and reactions the teen expresses. Don't tell the teen how he or she should or should not feel.

- Share your feelings with the teen. Allow the teen to comfort you.

- Offer warmth and your physical presence and affections.

- Be patient. Know that teens need to hear or tell "the story" and to ask the same questions over and over again.

- Reassure the teen that the loss is not contagious, that the death of one person does not mean that another loved one will also die or be injured.

- Maintain order, stability, and security in the teen's life.

- Take your own advice. Take care of yourself. If you're not OK, the teen can't be OK.

- Many counselors can assist in working through feelings.[2]

Standing by young people working through difficult circumstances can be rewarding, yet the work can be very taxing—and we must consciously take care of our own needs, or we won't be able to be there for the students when they need us. Those in ministry to youth are very giving people, and they often sacrifice their own health while trying to support the kids. A balance must be struck. We'll examine that in the next chapter.

6 SURVIVAL TIPS FOR ADULTS HELPING KIDS

When tragedy strikes in the lives of young people, adults can feel overwhelmed with feelings of inadequacy. Adults may fear, *What if I say the wrong thing? What if I make them feel worse? Will I even have words to say? How can I reach out to someone else in the midst of my own pain?* These are all common reactions when we're faced with the responsibility of helping those under our care.

I remember my emotions when I was called to counsel following the Columbine tragedy. The 20-minute drive seemed like an eternity. In my fears I prayed to God, *Lord, what do I say to these people? I don't want to say the wrong thing. Please give me the right words for each person.*[1] My dependence on God caused me to lean on Him for the words to say and what to do. I'm sure I didn't say everything perfectly, but my prayer was that God would cause those I helped to hear only what He knew would help them through their grief. When I got home that night, I e-mailed three of my closest friends and asked them to pray for me since I knew I would be counseling in the Columbine community for a few days.

At the end of the third day, after counseling one of the high school students at one of the elementary schools near Columbine, an overwhelming despair enveloped me. The sadness I saw in the children had been heart-wrenching. The staff's grief was unfathomable to me. How could I ever find the words to ease their pain? I wondered if anything I could say would help them. I went home that night feeling very inadequate. I had done the best I could, but would it ever be enough?

That night when I turned on my computer to check my e-mail, I was surprised to see I had 64 messages. The night before, after sending that e-mail on the day of the tragedy to my three friends requesting prayer, I had received 18 messages from people I didn't even know. Now, as I clicked through the 64 messages, tears welled up in my eyes as I realized that my request for prayer had been forwarded to others.

E-mail from persons across the country and world—people I never met—said they were praying for me. An assurance rose up within me reminding me that all I had to do was open my mouth, and God would speak through me the healing words people needed to hear. I went to sleep that night with a peace I had never felt.

God Will Give the Words to Say

In the following weeks I faced many questions and concerns from parents and from students. My friend Kim, an assistant youth minister in a nearby church, faced a related challenge one Sunday morning. The mother of one of the girls in the youth group had known one of the students who had been killed. That Sunday morning when she brought her daughter to youth group, the mom confessed that she was terrified to drop her daughter off, yet she was terrified to stay at church with her. She felt the fear rising up inside her, and she was concerned that she would be unable to hold it all together and be strong for her daughter. What kind of impact could it have on her daughter if she realized the fear her mother was experiencing? As this mother confessed her feelings to Kim, Kim prayed for the right words.

"You have at least three hours while Sunday School and church is going on, right?"

"Yes, about that," the mother replied.

"What are some ways you like to pamper yourself? What makes you feel good?" Kim asked.

"I'm a single mom; I rarely get to even think about that." She sighed. Then after thinking for a few seconds, she said, "I like to read a good book, take a bath, eat ice cream, hike, go for a drive."

"What would be the most feasible for you to do in the next three hours?"

"Well," she said, "I could take a hot bath, read a little, eat some ice cream."

Kim encouraged her. "That sounds great to me. Why don't you skip church this morning and go home and do those things and see how you feel? If you think it would be too difficult to come back and pick up your daughter when church is over, call me, and I'll drop her off on my way home."

The mom gave Kim a hug and said, "Thanks for listening. Thanks for the ideas."

The weeks following the shootings had been difficult for this mother. Her daughter was asking tough questions she couldn't answer. As a single mom, she had to be strong even though she felt afraid, and she didn't have any other adults at home to confide in about her fears and questions. She also didn't know how to reach out to the friend whose son was killed in the tragedy. She was trying to be all things to all people while she herself was feeling lonely and frightened, and her stress was so intense that it interfered with her ability to think rationally.

Three hours later, she caught Kim in the sanctuary. With a smile on her face, she said, "I feel so much better now. I feel some strength again, and I think I'm going to make it. Thanks for your help."

Kim's experience helped me know that God will give me wisdom and the words to say to those I'm trying to help. When a crisis occurs, there are a lot of hurting people with needs I don't know. God wants to reach out to them, and He'll help us know what to say. We can depend on Him and ask for His help.

When we go through training in crisis response, we can't possibly be taught the correct response to every situation we may face. We must learn as much as we can so that we can respond as well as possible. No training can completely prepare me for some of the tragedies I may face. My responsibility is to be accountable to becoming better equipped to do what's required of me in this work. God will provide the rest.

Take Care of Yourself

Just as I advised the mother in the above situation to take care of herself, it's extremely important for adults in leadership roles in responding to a crisis situation to see that their own needs are being met. I recently heard Dina Robke, a local therapist with considerable crisis response experience, share how necessary it is for crisis responders to take care of themselves. She referred to the speech we hear from the flight attendant before our flight leaves the ground, the one about cabin pressure changes during an emergency. The attendant explains the importance of parents' putting the oxygen masks on themselves first and then on their children. Only then can the parents be sure they'll be able to help their children. If a child gets an oxygen mask first, the parent may become incapacitated and unable to help the child.

It's the same for adults trying to help kids in this type of work. If adults become worn down by ignoring their own needs in their efforts to help others, they'll become depleted and incapable of effectively helping others. There are many needs in the midst of a crisis, and we must do all we can to meet all needs. But we can't do it at the expense of our own health.[2] There may even be a time that we must step aside from our roles for a while until we can regain our capacity to help at an effective level. That's why the team approach is extremely important in crisis response. If one person needs to take a break, then someone else can fill in during that time.

Another way to take care of ourselves is to do something physical. During a crisis, toxins build up in our bodies, and it's important to find ways to release those to avoid their detrimental effects on our physical and mental health. Physical activity can include walking, riding a bike, running, hiking, playing basketball, lifting weights, and so on.

It may be difficult to get away and take the time for physical activity, so look for opportunities to slip away for a five-minute walk around the church or school. If you can get exercise outside, that's even better. When you need to discuss plans with someone, instead of meeting in an office, have your discussion while taking a walk. Or walk around the outside of the building with a good buddy to check in with each other to see how you're both doing.

A counselor I know described the previous points as his strategy for coping with the effects of a tragedy at the school where he works: "My family's and my church group's prayers and support helped. I was able to get out and exercise on my bicycle the next morning. I read somewhere that it's important to exercise within the first 48 hours to get rid of some of the toxins."

Another obstacle to overcome during a crisis is finding time to spend alone with God. When you get up in the morning, your mind is often racing with everything that needs to be done. It may be difficult to sit quietly and concentrate on the Lord. Leaders are exhausted by the long hours they put in during a crisis. When you do get the opportunity to spend a few moments with God—even if it's not the usual length of time—have paper and pen handy to jot down thoughts that come to your mind that are off the subject of your quiet time.

Sometimes you may not have time for your devotions because every minute seems to be taken up dealing with the crisis. God understands, and He wants you to know He's right there with you in the midst of the busyness anyway. In your car you can put in a Bible-on-tape or CD, but don't expect that you'll be able to completely focus on the message, because your mind may be racing. Or put on some Christian music wherever you are. I'm amazed that when I'm the most stressed, a song will come on the radio to remind me that God is in control, that He'll equip me with everything I need for the situation, that He's there with His comfort and peace.

A key to taking care of ourselves is the support of friends and loved ones. Spend some time away from the crisis when possible to relieve some of the stress. After the first crucial days of the crisis, try to get away to spend some time with friends. Go on an excursion to a favorite place, eat at your favorite restaurant, or maybe watch a fun movie. If at all possible, try to get your mind off the crisis and think about other things.

As leaders, we also need someone to talk to whom we can trust to keep everything we share in strictest confidence. This can be a spouse, a significant other, a family member, a trusted friend, or a person of a similar leadership position elsewhere who's not involved in the crisis. It helps to share our fears, concerns, questions, and comments knowing that we won't be judged or critiqued. There can be so much pressure placed on our shoulders, and we may need a neutral party to confide in without worrying about his or her opinions of us or if we're saying the right thing. This person will be invaluable throughout the healing process in dealing with our own issues after the crisis.

Also, remember to eat right and get enough rest. We take these two things for granted in everyday life, but they need to be consciously adhered to as much as possible during stressful times of tragedy. During a major crisis, you may spend long hours counseling students who have been impacted. You may often get home late and not get adequate rest for days at a time. That's when it is important for you to grab a few minutes to relax and pray whenever you have a chance. Even if you have only ten minutes to renew your mind and soul, it will refresh you.

Eating right may be a challenge because you have to eat whenever you can fit it in. You may not be able to take time for lunch or dinner and may eat on the run. You may end up stopping at fast-food restaurants because you've missed the dinner hour or don't want to cook when you get home. After a few days of that, your overall sense of health and well-being will begin to suffer. If you must stop for fast food, at least choose a salad or some of the better choices on the menu.

It's OK to splurge a little on comfort foods during our crisis response endeavors unless they're detrimental to health. I love ice cream—it's one of my comfort foods. I allow myself to indulge in that a bit during times of high stress, knowing I may gain weight and need to make the effort to get it off later. But it's OK for a while.

Another way to take care of yourself is to make it a priority to attend crisis team debriefings that may be offered by mental health workers. These afford a time for each person to share how he or she is doing personally. A trained mental health professional in crisis debriefing (not someone on the crisis team) can help crisis team members process their own issues, questions, and fears so that their effectiveness is not compromised and stress does not compound to the point of a debilitating condition. Through this process you may realize there are some issues about the crisis that have deeply impacted you and need some attention. At times it could be helpful to get some counseling from a trained pastor or counselor.

As leaders, each of us has a responsibility to assess our ability to deal with the crisis—if we're too close to the situation, a family member is involved, and so on—and whether we'll be able to handle the incident at full capacity. At times, though, we may not be able to make that determination personally, and someone else must come forward and encourage us to step away for awhile. This is a sensitive topic, so it should be handled gently and with much prayer.

When Helping Hurts

In the last section we discussed the importance of taking care of ourselves. In a prolonged period of crisis response, even if we're doing everything we can to take care of ourselves, we can experience some detrimental effects. This does not indicate a weakness—it reveals that we have been impacted at a deep level. A result that can develop is known as "compassion fatigue." Continued trauma over an extended period of time can cause this condition. Compassion fatigue is becoming more common today for those in the helping professions, and not just with those who are part of a crisis response team. It occurs as a result of the toll taken on one's body after prolonged stress and lack of rest.

Compassion fatigue is a form of burnout that manifests itself as physical, emotional, and spiritual exhaustion. To recharge your batteries, you must first learn to recognize when you're wearing down and then get into the habit of doing something every day that will replenish you.[3] It's sad that in helping others we can hurt ourselves if we don't find a balance in our efforts. We must listen to others when they voice concerns that we're overextending ourselves. Sometimes we can become so tired that it's difficult to hear God's voice, and that's when we need to listen to those voices of loved ones and friends who have our best interests at heart.

Although the symptoms vary, the following red flags may indicate that you have compassion fatigue:

- anger
- blaming
- chronic lateness
- depression
- diminished sense of personal accomplishment
- exhaustion (physical or emotional)
- frequent headaches
- gastrointestinal complaints
- high self-expectations
- a sense of hopelessness
- hypertension
- inability to maintain balance of empathy and objectivity

- increased irritability
- less ability to feel joy
- low self-esteem
- sleep disturbances
- workaholism[4]

If you sense by this list that you may have compassion fatigue, here are some specific things you can do:

- find someone to talk to
- understand that the pain you feel is normal
- start exercising and eating properly
- get enough sleep
- take some time off
- develop other interests
- identify what's important to you[5]

The crisis team members should be made aware of these signs and symptoms of compassion fatigue. God has called us to these positions of influence among young people. When we take advantage of opportunities for training and learning, it helps us prepare for whatever crises may be ahead. God will bring the things we learn to our remembrance and help us each step of the way. He will give the wisdom for every situation we're in. We must do our part by being good stewards of our bodies and lives and taking care of ourselves.

7 SHORT-TERM RESPONSE: DAYS 3 THROUGH 7 FOLLOWING THE CRISIS

After the first couple of days of crisis, reality begins to settle in, the shock wears off, and new issues begin to surface. In chapter 4 we talked about the immediate response and listed each crisis team member's responsibilities. We'll begin this chapter in the same way, but we'll give some general information that will be valuable to you during this stage. In the Crisis Team Member Responsibilities section of your crisis team manual, add this information to what you included from chapter 4. Again, we'll start with the team manager.

Crisis Team Members' Responsibilities

Team Manager Responsibilities

- Facilitate crisis team meetings as needed. (Y/S)
- Facilitate staff meetings as necessary. (Y/S)
- Plan and facilitate a parent meeting. During the meeting, information can be released about what helps and resources are available to the youth, parents, and families. Any outreach plans for those deeply impacted can

also be discussed. This can also be a time to dispel rumors and give parents ideas on how to help their kids. (Y/S)

- Follow up as appropriate with the family of the victim/deceased, or designate other crisis team members to follow up. (Y/S)
- Work with the staff reps to follow up as needed with impacted staff members. (Y/S)
- Help the care-and-concern reps to continue providing counseling/support for the students. (Y/S)
- Give updates to the appropriate leaders/officials (church or school leaders, elders, board members, and so on). (Y/S)
- Coordinate with the communications rep the dissemination of information about the viewing/funeral/service. (Y/S)
- Work with the crisis team to arrange for representatives to attend the viewing and funeral. (Y/S)
- If possible, work with the care-and-concern reps to arrange for a place after the service where kids can gather to process their feelings, emotions, or grief, or just talk. (Y/S)
- Encourage parents to attend the viewing/funeral with their young people. If the kids want to be with their friends, advise the parents to stay nearby to observe how the kids are doing. (Y/S)
- Pursue any extra resources deemed necessary. (Y/S)
- Plan and facilitate the final staff meeting concerning the crisis. (Y/S)

- Arrange for an outside mental health professional to facilitate the final mandatory crisis team debriefing. (Y/S)
- Assign the clerical rep to write notes of appreciation to those who provided assistance. (Y/S)
- Set and facilitate a meeting to review the crisis plan and response efforts thus far with the crisis team. Make any necessary revisions to the plan and crisis team manual. (Y/S)
- Assign the clerical rep to make the corrections to the crisis team manual, and get copies to the crisis team. (Y/S)

Communications Rep Responsibilities

- Follow up as needed with impacted staff members. (Y/S)
- Coordinate with the team manager the dissemination of information about the viewing/funeral/service. (Y/S)
- Give updates to the appropriate leaders/officials. (Y/S)
- Pursue any extra resources deemed necessary. (Y/S)
- Help the team manager plan and implement the final staff meeting concerning the crisis. (Y/S)
- Help the team manager arrange for the final mandatory crisis team debriefing. (Y/S)
- Work with the clerical rep to write notes of appreciation to those who provided assistance. (Y/S)
- Give input on the revision of the crisis team manual. (Y/S)

Care-and-Concern Reps Responsibilities

- In talking with students about the viewing/wake and funeral/memorial service, find out if they've been to one before. Tell them what they can expect. Talk about what an open casket is and the feelings that may arise within them upon seeing a dead body. Tell them they don't need to view the body if they feel uncomfortable about it. If parents are attending the services, let them know they should be near their child when he or she approaches the open casket. Tell the parents their children may have nightmares after seeing the dead body. Also, let parents know their children may grieve differently than the parents do. Tell parents they should decide what is best for their children. For some, it may be important to go to the service, and for others it may not. Many students have told me that they wanted to go to a classmate's funeral but that their parents wouldn't allow it. As a church or school leader, you can have key input into those discussions among family members. If a student really wants to attend a funeral but the parent doesn't want to go, ask the parent if another trusted adult could be responsible for the student during the service. (Y/S)

- If possible, arrange for a place after the service where kids can gather to process their feelings, emotions, grief, or just talk. (Y/S)

- Encourage parents of the students to attend the viewing/funeral with their young people. If the kids want to be with their friends, that's all right. Parents should stay nearby to observe how the kids are doing. (Y/S)

- Work with the team manager to arrange for staff representatives to be present at the viewing and funeral. (Y/S)

- If there's a reason for concern, ask the family of the deceased to check in the casket for possible suicide notes put in by distraught students that might say such things as "I'll see you tomorrow" and so on. (See chapter 8.) (Y/S)

- Contact military branches with the name of the student so they don't make recruiting calls to the family. (S)

- Continue to monitor the needs of the staff and students, and provide or advocate for resources for them. (Y/S)

- Prepare leaders and students for the return of victims (in the case of accidents, hospitalizations, etc.) or highly impacted students—siblings and so on. This can be done informally, one-on-one, or in small groups, and there also should be conversation about the students' return in their classrooms. Help the kids know what to expect if there are changes in the returning student, such as a wheelchair, visible changes in appearance, scars, and so on. Talk to them about the tendency to stare at the injured areas and to be aware of when they're doing it so they can try to stop. Tell them not to ignore the student but to try a simple phrase such as "I'm sorry for what you've been through. I don't know what to say, but I want you to know I care about you." Let them know that sometimes it's OK to just sit with their friend and not say anything. Encourage the kids to ask the student if he or she would like some assistance if they see him or her struggling. Tell them not to simply start helping but to ask first. Impacted students need to feel a sense of independence if they've lost any part of their normal functioning abilities. They may feel offended if people try to help them in ways in which they're capable of taking care of themselves. Help dispel rumors of the returning youth's condition. Sometimes rumors fly about injuries being contagious or an injury in one area affecting other areas of functioning. Make sure you have the parents' permission to talk about their son's or daughter's condition prior to these conversations. Sometimes it helps if the parent comes in and talks to the group or class with or without the student present before the actual first day back. (Y/S)

- If needed, provide student support groups and/or staff support groups. (Y/S)
- Send notes of appreciation to those who provided assistance. (Y/S)
- Help plan and attend the final crisis team debriefing. (Y/S)
- Give input on the revision of the crisis team manual. (Y/S)

Staff Reps Responsibilities

- Continue contact with highly impacted staff members, and advocate for their needs. (Y/S)

- Continue to monitor needs of staff members, and relay those to the crisis team. (Y/S)
- Send notes of appreciation to those who provided assistance. (Y/S)
- Attend the final crisis team debriefing. (Y/S)
- Give input on the revision of the crisis team manual. (Y/S)

Clerical Rep Responsibilities

- Get information from the communications rep and team manager to help write notes of appreciation to those who provided assistance. (Y/S)
- Attend the final crisis team debriefing. (Y/S)
- File all documentation of the crisis in the appropriate places. (Y/S)
- Give input on and make the revisions to the crisis team manual as recommended by the crisis team, and distribute copies to the team. (Y/S)
- Copy new packets for the initial crisis team meeting for the next crisis. (Incident Report Form, Students/Staff Impacted by the Incident, and the Crisis Team Member Responsibilities.) (Y/S)

Facilities Rep Responsibilities

- If the facilities have been affected by the crisis, continue maintenance efforts to restore the facility to the original condition as much as possible. (Y/S)
- Make any necessary changes to the facilities indicated by the needs that arose during the crisis that affected or

hindered the effectiveness of the response by emergency personnel or other parties. (Y/S)

- Make recommendations for the revision of the crisis team manual from lessons learned from the most recent crisis. (Y/S)
- Attend the final crisis team debriefing. (Y/S)

Parent Rep Responsibilities

- Encourage parents to attend the viewing/funeral with their children. (Y/S)
- Relay parental concerns/needs to the crisis team members. (Y/S)
- Help the team manager plan a parent meeting. (Y/S)
- Help coordinate continued outreach efforts to families impacted by the crisis. (Y/S)
- Make recommendations to the crisis team for improving future response efforts. (Y/S)

Student Rep Responsibilities

- Relay student concerns and needs to the crisis team members. (Y/S)
- Help with the outreach efforts to the students impacted by the crisis. (Y/S)
- Make recommendations to the crisis team about what can make future response efforts more effective. (Y/S)

Building a Caring Community

The most important thing a church or school can do in the aftermath of a crisis is to help build a caring environment among its youth, parents, staff, and community. Some deliberate steps must be taken to address the needs of all the people impacted by the crisis. The following are some ideas that might be helpful to your church or school if a student has committed suicide.

Encourage the students to let you know if their friends are struggling. It is common to learn that students who commit suicide have voiced their plans to friends. But kids tend to feel one of the worst things they could do is betray a confidence. That is considered "tattling." There is an unspoken rule among teens that they will never tell adults of their serious problems—but they will tell their friends.

You can change the climate of the school to the notion that informing an adult about a hurting friend could save your friend's life. Establish a "confidential tip box" in the counseling office where students can place the names and any other information concerning their friends. Another way to aid in this effort is to create something called a Courage-to-Call card that is the size of a business card. On the front of it put information on who a student could talk to if he or she or a friend is struggling. On the back put Tips for Tough Times with bullets of information on how the student can take care of himself or herself or help others during tough times. A sample of the card is found in chapter 12.

The best way to get this information out to all students is through classroom presentations. A counselor and a student council member can go into each English class in the school. Every student attends an English class, so you will catch each student that way. As you talk with the classes, you will learn some valuable information. Here are some of the topics to cover:

- We've been through a very difficult time as a school—a student who was walking through our halls a short time ago is gone and will never be back. We'll never be the same.

- We want each of you to know we care about you. You may not think that or haven't seen a lot of evidence to support that, but the staff members at our school are here because they care about you. They could be making a lot more money working at other jobs, but they're here because they care about young people. If you don't believe that there is at least one staff member here who cares about you, we challenge you to look closer. Maybe you don't know any of the staff members very well, so you don't know if any of them care about you. We encourage you to get involved in a club or activity. Look for any staff members who take extra time to help you or are here extra hours doing their work. They do care about you.

- We've heard that the students who committed suicide had mentioned it to at least one friend. If you're that friend, we want you to know we support you and want to help you. It can be a tough thing to live with the rest of your life, and we want to help you. We want to encourage all of you to let a counselor or staff member know if you're ever concerned about any of your friends.

There are some heavy things you all deal with as teenagers. Let us help you with issues that are so tough that your friends don't know how to help you cope. Your friends can walk with you through the process, but get help from someone who is trained in those tough issues. We want to help you get through it all so we will still have you around walking these halls. If a friend confides something too difficult for you to handle, don't put pressure on yourself to keep a confidence about something you aren't qualified to deal with.

At this point in one of the presentations at a school where my colleague works, a student said, "If I tell, my friend may get mad at me."

Immediately, without a delay, the student council member with my colleague said, "I used to think that too. Dana was a friend of mine, and now I've realized that I would rather have a mad friend than a dead friend. Even if she had never talked to me again, I would rather have her living and not speaking to me than realizing that because I never told, I will never be able to talk to her again anyway. I have to live the rest of my life with that regret. It's not worth it!"

Every student in that class got the point, and there was a silence in the room that comes only from a life-altering realization of the value of life and friendship. The students got the message loud and clear.

You may receive several confidential tips a day for a few weeks. Follow up as appropriate. As the kids see how you respond to the confidential tips, they will begin to trust you.

The students learn to walk through tough times with their friends with the help of the adults.

We made posters from the information on the Courage-to-Call Cards, and we hung them around the school. The student council even went out into the community to ask some business owners to put the posters up so the students would see that they cared about them too. Many business owners said yes.

Information is important to youth and to adults. You probably have some brochures and information on hand right now that would be good to hand out during a time of crisis. Your students have probably heard talks or lessons on the subject of getting through tough times. Your staff has probably given Bible studies on biblical characters who faced adversity. It may be a good idea to create handouts with some of that information and have copies available in the office so the kids can have access to them. The parents will be glad to have them available as well.

Handouts or brochures are helpful on other subjects also, such as parent issues, relationship issues, peer pressure, identity issues, and so on. These brochures should be available all year in places where other students won't be watching to see who takes the brochures. That will help the kids feel comfortable that when the need arises they know where to get some help.

This short-term response stage can be exhausting. A week after the crisis, reality begins to settle in as everyone realizes how his or her life will be different as a result of the situation. Some are more deeply impacted than others. Some who didn't seem to be impacted at all may begin to show signs of the effects on them personally. Everyone reacts differently to trauma, and that's why as a leader you must always be attentive to what's going on around you. The crisis team members must be watchful to see and address needs that arise.

Throughout the crisis response process are unique issues that youth groups and Christian schools face. From the immediate response to the short-term response, within the first week of the crisis are so many pressing needs that have to be addressed that inevitably different circumstances will crop up that will take the crisis team by surprise. Even though some issues youth groups face are not the same as Christian schools will face, it's good to be familiar with all possible scenarios since churches and schools (even public schools) need to work together in times of crisis. It's an important way a community can come together to help those in need. It's a great chance to make a positive difference in their surroundings. We'll discuss some of these unique issues in the next chapter.

8 UNIQUE ISSUES IN CRISIS RESPONSE

"Donna, can you talk to Lindsey? I know she's not one of your students, but since you're a Christian, you may understand the questions she's asking." The attendance secretary brought a frail girl into the counselor's office. With tears streaming down her face, Lindsey sunk into the chair and sobbed even more.

"Lindsey," Donna said, trying to start the conversation. "Can you tell me the reason for your tears?"

She whispered, "I let God down. He counted on me, and I let Him down. And David isn't here anymore." She gasped through her tears. "Why didn't I say more? Why didn't I say more? God counted on me. I messed up, and now David's gone!"

Realizing that Lindsey knew David, who had committed suicide the night before, added an extra weight of heaviness to her comments. This could be a turning point in her faith in God. What Donna said could turn her toward God or farther away from Him. Donna prayed silently, *Lord, please help me! Please give me your strength and the right words.*

Donna began. "Lindsey, tell me what happened."

Peering through her tears, she replied, "With one minute left in class, I started talking with David. He asked me what I did over the weekend. I said I went to church. He asked if I read the Bible every day. I said, 'Most days, but not every day.'"

Wiping her tears, she continued: "Next he said, 'I went to church once, but that was a long time ago.' At that instant the bell rang, and we went our separate ways. I should have said more. That was probably his last chance to hear about God. Maybe he wouldn't have killed himself."

Donna prayed, *Lord, what are your words for Lindsey?* He gave Donna a perspective she hadn't thought of before.

"Lindsey, when David asked you what you did over the weekend, what went through your mind?"

"I knew I should mention church, but I was afraid he and his friends would make fun of me."

"But did you say it anyway?" Donna asked.

"Yes," she replied.

"So you knew he might make fun of you, but you said it anyway?"

Lindsey said, "Yes, I did," obviously irritated at Donna for asking it again.

"Lindsey, God knew there was one minute left in class. If He had wanted you to say more, He would have caused your conversation to start earlier. You said exactly what God wanted you to say. He used you to remind David about God and His love for him. We don't know what happened in David's life in the hours between your conversation with him and his suicide. I believe God divinely used you to remind David of His love for him. God was still reaching out to him up to his last hours before he made that fatal decision to take his own life."

Lindsey blinked to clear her tears. Donna continued.

"Lindsey, God picked you to say those brief comments about Him, because He knew you would be faithful and strong enough to say those words. God handpicked you, and you were faithful. Since you were faithful in that one-minute conversation, God knows you will be faithful with similar situations in the future. It's a privilege to know you, Lindsey."

They continued their conversation for a few more minutes. Grinning, Lindsey thanked Donna and gave her a big hug.

This was one of the most unique counseling sessions Donna ever had. The pressure she felt in knowing that this was a faith-impacting moment in Lindsey's life is one of the greatest weights she had ever felt in her counseling career. She's been in youth ministry and women's ministry for more than 30 years, and never felt such pressure. Lindsey had even been feeling suicidal over this.

It was amazing when God gave Donna the wisdom of what to say. We all have regrets about not saying something or saying the wrong thing to people, but she knew this could be a life-or-death situation. She had not thought in terms of some of the specifics that God brought to her mind that day.

In this arena of crisis response, some unique issues or circumstances can catch us off guard. That's why we must be completely dependent on God for wisdom that only He can give. Even if you've been a counselor for a while and involved in crisis response in some intense situations, there is still a lot to learn. In this chapter we'll talk about some things that don't exactly fit nicely anywhere else in the book, but I think they're important enough to share with you. We'll start with a topic you'll face in the immediate response phase.

The Empty Chair

We mentioned the empty chair in chapter 4. This occurs with the death of one young person. At school it's obvious that there will be an empty chair or desk in each classroom he or she was in. But in your youth group meetings there may be a chair the person sat in on a regular basis. That can become an ominous sight for the kids if it's not addressed openly. It's important not to remove the chair or make it disappear. If it's easier to just move it to the side of the room, that's fine. Some people may recommend making a new seating chart in the school classroom, which may work in some cases but not all. Each teacher or leader should ask the kids what they feel most comfortable with, letting them know that if their first choice doesn't work as they had hoped, they can change their decision.

We recommend putting a box on the empty chair or desk in which the young people can place notes to the family of the person who died. They can also write a note to that person saying what he or she meant to them. It's important to prevent the chair from becoming a shrine. All that's necessary on the chair is the box, and if the kids want to decorate the box, that's OK.

It's recommended for the leaders (typically the care-and-concern reps) to read the notes before giving them to the family. This precautionary measure is necessary in case there are any notes blaming family members or notes containing personal vendettas against family members for perceived mistreatment of the deceased. We don't want to introduce more trauma to the family.

When the box has been taken off the chair, in the case that the seating chart hasn't changed, let the chair become a catch-all. Maybe put a stapler or tape dispenser on it. That way it becomes a useful space instead of going back to an empty chair again. Sometimes even when a seating chart has been changed, kids may say, "That's the seat that _____ [the deceased] used to sit in. I wonder if it's cursed." Those are irrational thoughts, but that's the way some kids think. So sometimes just changing the seating chart may not work. Maybe changing the way the chairs are arranged will help. For example, instead of rows, try moving the chairs into a circle. The young people can give you valuable input on what works for them.

Recommendations for Services

A funeral or memorial service typically takes place within a week after the death instead of the first two days—the immediate response period. Yet planning for the service takes place in the immediate response stage, so you must be aware of some considerations you may want to suggest if the family seeks your input for your youth group members or students from school.

Usually the family is at the mercy of the funeral home as to the time of the service. But if there's an option, it's helpful if the service can be in the afternoon or after school hours. The reason for this is that many students will have to miss school to attend the service, and that can put more stress on them. Also, parents won't have to miss a day of work to attend the service, and you want as many parents to attend as possible. Also, if the service is in the morning, many students may not go back to school, and the parents will have to deal with their skipping school and so on.

Another recommendation regarding services is not to have an open mike situation in which anyone can go to the microphone and speak. At a couple of student funerals, we have seen a "one-upmanship" develop between the teens during the open-mike time. One student said that he was the deceased's best friend, then the next would imply he was a better friend because they did such and such together, and the cycle continued. The focus became who was the deceased's better friend instead of the virtues of the person who died. Instead of an open mike, we now recommend that the family pick two or three close friends and a leader or teacher to speak at the service. This provides a more controlled atmosphere, and the focus stays on the student who has died.

Earlier we mentioned checking for notes in the casket.

Sometimes people slip notes into the casket of the deceased. We encourage checking the notes if there's concern there are students who are so distraught they could think of taking their lives just to be with their deceased friend. This may sound harsh, but sometimes it's necessary. Make sure you get the family's permission. When the casket is wheeled out at the end of the service and taken directly to the burial site, there typically isn't a chance to check the notes in the casket. The most opportune time is after the viewing the day before the funeral. This is a delicate matter, so pray about it and ask the opinion of others in leadership before asking the family for permission.

Memorials

Another subject that may spring up is that of a memorial to the student. The kids may want to make T-shirts with the youth's picture on them or may want to plant a tree on the property. There are many factors to consider in this situation, and they must be dealt with gently, because the kids have good intentions. The problem with planting a tree is—what happens if there are several deaths that year? Will you plant more trees? Also, if the tree dies prematurely, it will be traumatic. The matter of the T-shirt is complicated and deals with the topic of death and may slow the healing process for the students.

If a student is lonely or feeling left out and sees the response that's put forth for someone else who has died, he or she may think, *If I die, they'll put my picture on their shirts or plant a tree in my name.* The student may think he or she will be more important in death than in life. In the case of a suicide death, we must be careful not to glorify the suicide. All deaths should be treated the same.

What we recommend in place of a memorial is something away from the church or school building. Some students checked with authorities at a park they frequented and got permission to buy a bench with a nameplate in memory of the deceased student. It's now a place where the kids can meet together and reminisce. That's an option if young people insist on creating a memorial somewhere. It should be entirely the students' project, though.

Youth Directors Assisting Public Schools

Typically youth directors have a good relationship with Christian schools. They're usually welcomed with open arms and are considered resources for various needs at the school— chapel or classroom speakers, chaperones at activities, and so on. Yet often youth directors have some hesitation in approaching a public school for various reasons. Many public school administrators have preconceived notions of youth directors' intentions to proselytize the students. It's sad to say that a few well-intentioned but misinformed youth directors may have closed doors to public schools by inappropriate methods of interacting with public school officials.

Some of the misconceptions public school officials have of church workers is that (1) they'll try to force students to accept and follow their own views of God, (2) they'll attempt to brainwash kids to their way of thinking, or (3) they'll incite rage and anger on campus by their very presence.

If you're a youth worker and want to forge a partnership with public schools in your area, you must first search your heart and evaluate your intentions. If your attitude is that you're going to "save the school," there will be an automatic turn-off in the school official's mind. If you genuinely care about the school official as a person and a partner in helping kids, then that will come across clearly. Know there may be "red flags" in that person's mind during your first few meetings because of previous experiences or stories he or she has heard. If the school administrator is a Christian, he or she will probably be more receptive to you but must adhere to policies of which you may not be aware.

It's imperative that you know that administrators face liability and ethical issues by allowing you on campus. If students feel you're forcing a belief on them that they or their parents don't agree with, then the administrator, school, and district could be sued. The administrator would most likely lose his job and administrator's license too. So the administrator is risking a lot by putting his or her trust in you.

You must realize that you'll be expected to operate within the school official's rules and parameters. There should never be a "we vs. they" attitude or a "holier than thou" attitude. If that's the case, you must pray diligently for that to change in you. If Jesus were in your shoes, how would He treat a public school administrator? If you feel you have some attitudes that may get in the way of your efforts, then I recommend that you find a public school official in your church or in a nearby church and sit down and talk with him or her before you attempt to approach a similar person you want to reach out to. Your efforts will greatly impact school administrators' views of the students in their school from your youth group. So a lot is at stake in your dealings with school administrators.

The key is that you must act with integrity and sincerity in all that you do. If the administrator senses your authenticity, he or she knows you can be trusted. You must hold yourself accountable to act in the best interests of all involved. That being said, how do you forge a partnership with public school officials?

First, approach the person from the standpoint that what happens in the school will affect your kids and that what happens in your church will impact his or her kids. Let the administrator know that you want to form a positive relationship so that when a crisis occurs you'll be a resource to help meet the needs of the students. Emphasize that you'll adhere to the parameters set forth and that you won't take advantage of situations to the detriment of students.

A fear in a lot of administrators' minds will be that you'll want to recruit kids for your church during a time of weakness and crisis. Many have images of brainwashing maniacs in their minds about youth workers. So your reassurance of your pure motives in partnering to meet kids' needs is important. You should make sure that in reaching out to kids you leave God out of the conversation on school grounds and in other situations where it's not the student's choice to be there.

It would be important to talk with the official about what's appropriate—if you can mention your church and so on. This is a very sensitive topic, and you must honor the official's wishes, or the door may close and you may never get to be involved again. Many officials will allow youth directors on campus to talk only with their own youth group members, while other schools have banned church youth workers of any kind on campus. The concern is that if they allow Christian workers on the campus, they must also allow workers from other churches in direct conflict with the Christian faith. Whatever the school official's decision is, you must adhere to it completely. So if the school officials say they would like to form a partnership with you, then what should be the next step?

It would be good to have several meetings in which you discuss the school crisis plan and the needs of the kids in the time of crisis. It should be a free flow of conversation with a give-and-take of ideas. Again, in the school setting, the school official has the last word. Some things you can talk about for crisis situations at the school are the needs of the school, students, and staff, and any resources you can provide.

Find out what needs the school has that you can play a role in meeting. You can share some insights you've gained through your experience or this book. As the school official is talking, you can bring up some points you think of that may not have been addressed in his or her crisis plan. As the administrator sees that you've put a lot of thought into the crisis response process with your own youth group, your input will be valued to a greater degree. You can talk about your own process of planning and exploring in developing your crisis plan.

Another need that may arise is an alternative site, besides the school, for evacuations and so on. In some cases a site separate from the school for meetings and other activities is needed. You can offer your church building for an emergency meeting site. You may be able to offer chairs, tables, or other items if needed.

Some administrators may allow you to be available to the school staff. If that's the case, you may be allowed to hang out in the staff lounge. There you may spend your time talking about the weekend football game, a recent concert, or a variety of other things and may never get to talk about God. That needs to be acceptable to you. You can be a support without ever mentioning God. You can build genuinely caring relationships that will bless you while you're blessing others. Once you build that trust, if they have an interest in spiritual things, they'll bring them up.

Another way to support the administrator is by letting him or her know what resources you can provide the students and staff. Maybe your church could provide food for meetings or the workers during the crisis. It was helpful during the intense aftermath of the deaths of three students at the school where I work when people brought in food and water for us. As workers, we didn't have time to stop and make our lunch or heat it up. It was nice to have sandwiches, fruit, vegetables, and other goodies right there for us to grab between tasks.

If the school needs extra hands to fold letters, staple forms, and so on, that's a good way to help, because often staff is shorthanded because of the extra duties that surface in the midst of the crisis. There are many ways you or your church can be of help to a school if they've learned they can trust you and your motives. It's always vital to remember that one breach of confidence by you or someone else attached to your group will slam shut doors that may never open again. So whoever you include in your support efforts must be accountable and must also be persons you trust implicitly to stay within the boundaries that have been set.

To maintain this relationship, it's important to meet together as needed to keep the relationship ties strong. A friendship such as this can benefit the kids as well both parties involved. There must be no secret, underlying motives, because they'll surface in times of stress that come with a crisis, and then the damage may be irreparable.

I was encouraged to hear of one community of churches that was able to accomplish this type of outreach very effectively. I recently met an owner of a bookstore in Iowa. He told me about a collaboration he was a part of several years ago. It developed from a Pastors' Prayer Fellowship when he was a pastor at a church in another state. Fifteen pastors were involved in the fellowship, and their outreach to the public school principals in their area forged trusting partnerships and relationships between the churches and schools. Their example is one that could be replicated throughout the country.

A similar bond was created with our schools. After three deaths in a short amount of time at the school where I work, a church called to ask what it could do to help. I mentioned how many students needed counseling but couldn't afford it. They raised $4,000, and we were able to get help for kids who needed it. The effort has continued, and last year they raised more than $100,000, and the fund—The Second Wind Fund—has grown to reach out to schools in our district and others by helping more than 450 kids get the help they needed. Great things can come from effective partnerships.

Christian Schools Collaborating

A tragedy cripples a school in many ways. Staff members will be directly impacted and may be put out of commission unless someone is trained to step in. Whether it's a minor event or a tragedy that shuts down the whole school, help is needed to put the pieces back together. What better group could there be to help than another school? In a metropolitan region there's usually a number of other Christian schools in the area. If you have at least one other Christian school nearby, you may want to strongly consider a partnership in crisis response. The more schools involved, the better it will be in the event one of the schools is not able to participate for some reason at any given time. What can an areawide crisis response collaboration offer?

One school district has one representative from each school on a districtwide crisis team. There are many schools in the district, so only one representative from each school is needed. If you have fewer schools in your area, you may need two or more representatives from each school. That would be a group decision made by the administrators.

Some duties of the areawide crisis responders can include roaming the hallways and school grounds to find struggling kids to be escorted to the office for help. Counselors or mental health workers can help with counseling, and staff members could be in the office to assist with clerical duties. An extra administrator can help with security or parent relations. The jobs can be as varied as the types of crises.

The areawide crisis responders will require training in their duties and responsibilities. This will require the communication of general information about all schools to those involved. A school should have the option of not participating in a crisis response effort if there's a need to keep its own personnel at its own school site. That's why each member on this team may not be called for each event. There needs to be a rotation of members assigned to respond to each crisis with designated backups appointed.

The members need to be trained in crisis response with an understanding of trauma and tragedy and other important crisis information like those discussed in this book. Members have the option of determining their ability to respond to a crisis at another school. Also, as with members of a school crisis team, members of the areawide collaboration need to be provided with badges designating them as such.

Besides schools, areawide crisis responders can also be beneficial for churches. It would be best to have these from churches as a whole and not youth groups—meaning they would consist of adults. These types of teams can be a lifeline to a church or school in need. Having people in your position from another church or school who can understand and support you means a lot. You know they can relate to what you're feeling and going through, so a measure of strength comes from that knowledge. Also, those people are usually the ones you can go to later to help you process your own issues from the crisis. There's an unspoken understanding between people in a crisis response effort that no one else may ever understand. They can also be very helpful in praying for you during the healing process. These types of people are a godsend during very intense times of crisis and can become close friends.

Crisis response can be a devastating experience in the throes of grief and loss. It's important to understand and prepare for unique issues you may face. Then the weight of the impact can be lessened as you're empowered by knowledge from the experiences of others. Collaboration with others can offer hope, and when you face the long-term response phase, you'll have the courage to keep pressing on. We see the light at the end of the tunnel, and life begins to return to our church or school. The "postvention" stage is where the healing truly begins.

9 LONG-TERM RESPONSE:
THE SECOND WEEK AND BEYOND

Once the crisis has subsided, the work isn't over. There can be many residual effects on the youth group or school that leaders should watch for. As in chapter 7, we begin with a delineation of crisis team members' responsibilities and will then address other aspects of the "postvention" stage.

"Postvention" is the time after the intervention stage and consists of strategies and activity concerns that surface after a crisis. In this stage, adjustments can be made to cover issues that may have fallen through the cracks in the prevention and intervention stages.

Team Manager Responsibilities

- Arrange for meetings with various community entities that responded to the crisis and ask for suggestions on changes needed for a better response next time. (Y/S)
- Update all those in supervisory positions above you as to the effectiveness of the response and recommendations for changes. (Y/S)
- Create opportunities for support, encouragement, and

rejuvenation for yourself in the aftermath of the stress and pressure of the crisis. In other words, take care of yourself. (Y/S)

• Periodically check on those deeply impacted by the crisis. (Y/S)

• Monitor how the crisis team is doing and determine if it needs anything to help members cope with the aftermath of the crisis. (Y/S)

• Make notes of any updates that are needed to the crisis team manual, and present them at the next crisis team meeting. The crisis team should meet at the beginning and end of each year to review and make changes to the crisis team manual in accordance with the recommendations put forth by the crisis team. (Y/S)

• Get input from crisis team members to anticipate possible anniversary reactions. If applicable, assign the care-and-concern reps with the task of planning anniversary activities. (Y/S)

Communications Rep Responsibilities

• Tie up loose ends on any communication pieces that still need to be completed. (Y/S)

• Check with the clerical rep to confirm that all documentation of the crisis is filed in appropriate places. (Y/S)

• Make notes of updates needed to the crisis team manual, and present them at the next crisis team meeting. (Y/S)

- If applicable, communicate anniversary activities to the staff and students. (Y/S)

Care-and-Concern Reps Responsibilities

- Monitor student needs throughout the next several months, and provide follow-up activities as needed. (Y/S)
- If necessary, provide short- or long-term student support groups and/or staff support groups. (Y/S)
- Anticipate anniversary reactions, and (if applicable) plan anniversary activities. (Y/S)
- Make notes of updates needed to the crisis team manual, and present them at the next crisis team meeting. (Y/S)

Staff Reps Responsibilities

- Monitor staff needs throughout the next several months, and convey concerns or follow-up deemed necessary to crisis team members. (Y/S)
- Make notes of updates needed to the crisis team manual, and present them at the next crisis team meeting. (Y/S)

Clerical Rep Responsibilities

- File all documentation of the crisis in the appropriate places. (Y/S)
- Make notes of updates needed to the crisis team manual, and present them at the next crisis team meeting. (Y/S)

- Prior to the next year, update and make copies of the corrections and additions to the crisis team manual for distribution at the first crisis team meeting. (Y/S)

Parent Rep Responsibilities

- Monitor parental needs throughout the next several months, and convey concerns or follow-up deemed necessary to crisis team members. (Y/S)
- Make recommendations for revisions in the crisis plan as appropriate. (Y/S)

Student Rep Responsibilities

- Monitor student needs throughout the next several months and convey concerns or follow-up deemed necessary to crisis team members. (Y/S)
- Make recommendations for revisions in the crisis plan as appropriate. (Y/S)

The long-term response covers the period from two weeks after the crisis and beyond. The first step in knowing what to do is the assessment of needs of all those in your ministry. Once you've determined the needs, you will know what you have to implement to address all issues. Then the crisis team and staff can get to work to find out what training, programs, and resources are necessary to address the areas of concern for the crisis team, staff, students, and parents. The first step is the assessment of needs.

Assessment of Needs

The most important thing to do throughout the "postvention" stage is the continuous assessment of the needs of the young people, staff, and parents. This can be done in several ways—either formally through surveys or informally through observations. Keeping a pulse on how everyone is doing will determine the steps taken in this stage.

Formal assessment can occur through surveys given to each of the groups mentioned above. The formulation of the survey should be done with the appropriate reps from the crisis team or other key representatives within each group. You can create a simple survey with questions such as these:

- After the crisis, how are you doing personally?
- Do you have any questions for the crisis team about the way the crisis was handled?
- What has been the most difficult thing for you during this crisis?
- What would have helped you most during the crisis?
- How can we help you now?
- What needs do you see in your friends or loved ones that we need to address?
- As a result of this crisis, are there any topics you have questions about or would like to see covered in classes, group meetings, and so on?
- What do you think would help our group/school heal from this crisis?

These are some questions that will stir up valuable feedback for the crisis team and the rest of the staff in learning what your people need. Dialogue and observations can offer valuable input too. The assessment of needs will help drive your efforts to make sure valuable energy and time are not needlessly spent on unnecessary activities. The first thing you have to look at is the types of training that would help in areas that have been identified as lacking.

Training

Reviewing the response to the crisis will help determine what kinds of training would be beneficial for your group. It's important to consider the needs of all those in your care. The first group you should examine is the crisis team.

What were the weak areas of the crisis plan? Were they the result of weaknesses in the crisis plan or lack of training for the crisis team members? Once these things are considered, the next step is to find out what training is available for those areas. Do you need to consult experts in the medical field or emergency response system? Is it possible that crisis team members have been placed in roles not suitable to their personalities or expertise? Do you need to consult other churches or schools that have experienced this type of crisis? The answers to these questions will help determine what training if any is needed for your crisis team.

Training for your staff is crucial at all stages. Did your staff know their roles in the crisis plan? What areas need to be reviewed? Should there be any changes in the staff roles in the crisis plan? Is there any information that will help them more effectively carry out their duties next time? Do any problem areas need to be addressed? Many of these types of concerns can be discussed in a staff meeting. The staff may also need training from medical, emergency response, or mental health professionals too. Any areas of concern must be addressed. If they're not, the staff may lack confidence necessary to carry out their responsibilities during the next crisis.

Is there training that would help the students in the aftermath of the crisis? Would training be beneficial for all youth or just a handful who are in positions of leadership? Should more students be trained to help or have a designated role in emergency situations? In adversity, some students will show amazing abilities to work well under stress. You may want to find a key role in which to assign them for future situations. What training will they need in order to carry out their responsibilities?

How about the parents? Do they need training for a similar situation in the future? Can the parent reps use help in their efforts of monitoring parental concerns? Do they have enough training in their areas of responsibility? Is there a need for more volunteers to be recruited and trained?

Formal or informal training may be used for equipping your people. This can be large- or small-group training or one-on-one sessions. The trainers can be local or national specialists or people in your church or school who have expertise in the areas being addressed. Once training is acquired, then programs will be of help in implementing the concepts or initiatives presented.

Following the suicides of two students at a school in the eastern part of the state, in-services were provided for the staff to discuss and process the deaths and the residual effects on the school. Those times were also used for bonding in the midst of the fear, grief, and questions. It was a very valuable use of time, even though the time could have been used for more academic matters.

A specialist on the topic of suicide came to train administrators, counselors, and staff in separate meetings. That helped each of the groups understand the magnitude of the situation and the gravity of the situation. The training provided tools to use in working with the students, and it cleared up some myths that were hindering effectiveness in addressing the issue. Even though it cost money to bring in trainers, it was worth the investment, because it helped not only the kids but also the adults.

Many staff members also attended a workshop on suicide intervention. It featured practical training in the area of suicide prevention. Training of this type is available in many communities, and I encourage taking advantage of these opportunities. If funding is an issue, let your parent group know of the need, and they may be able to help provide funds for the training.

Parent nights can also help the parents with some of the concerns they have. Workshops on suicide prevention, how to communicate with kids, substance abuse, and other issues of relevance to parents and teens are also helpful. You most likely have parents or other adults associated with your church or school who may have expertise in these or similar subjects. Parent nights are extremely valuable, because they not only get out pertinent information regarding parenting issues but also provide parents with the opportunity to network with other parents.

Programs

Countless programs across the country and world on various topics can be useful in working with young people. To find programs relevant to your circumstances, you can go to youth ministry or school organization Web sites and publications. Church youth directors are experts at finding these types of programs. I encourage school personnel to contact local youth directors for some ideas if you have trouble finding programs.

The crisis that impacts your students will probably cause some peripheral issues to surface. Some of those issues may include drinking and driving, road rage, reckless driving, suicide, abuse, cancer, cutting (self-mutilation), eating disorders, and so on. In these cases adults must embrace these teachable moments to provide some direction, encouragement, and teaching on these issues. Many youth ministry organizations and publications can help with their publications and Web sites. Many school and community contacts (spiritual and secular) address topics you'll face while working in crisis situations. We've listed some of those organizations in the "Recommended Resources" section at the back of this book.

Other programs that may be of help in a school are support groups of one form or another. These can be small-group Bible studies, discipleship groups, cell groups, or traditional support groups. Following a crisis, it may help to start a group for those most highly impacted by the crisis. The issues these kids face are intense and may be too difficult for others not as highly impacted. Careful thought must go into creating these types of support groups following a crisis, and some of the above organizations can help in this area.

Resources

Following a crisis, resources of many different forms are needed to address various topics. These may be people and materials. Often people become discouraged, thinking they can't afford resources for their students. Besides the resources in your own church or school, you may be surprised by what's available. In a time of need, you may receive offers of help from unexpected sources. You should think through in advance how you'll address these types of offers.

On the day of a large-scale crisis at a school in a southern state, 35 counselors were on the scene at the elementary school where students were directed to report. An hour later there were about 100, and about an hour and a half later there were more than 250 counselors. Later, it was discovered that some media people had posed as counselors to gain entry into the school. As a church or school, you must process what you can do to ward off unwanted visitors.

People who can be a great resource to your church or school are experts in an area of need for your group. In the previous scenario, opportunistic people invaded the school's and students' privacy. An encouraging balance to that behavior is that reputable people will generously offer their time for your cause. Retired staff members can volunteer to fill in where there is a need. If there's damage to your facilities, often community members will volunteer their time and expertise to help rebuild the structure. Sometimes high-profile people are touched by your tragedy and may lend their names or talents to help raise funds for your cause. Some people have very loving hearts and give generously in the midst of crises.

Another type of resource available to you is materials of various kinds that are needed in the time of crisis. A tangible way people can help is by providing food, clothing, blankets, and so on, as we've seen with tragedies worldwide and nationwide involving tsunamis, hurricanes, and earthquakes. In recent years people have given money in record amounts. If you experience a crisis in your group or school—at home or on the road—you'll be amazed at the number of people who want to help. If you need resources, it's important to get the word out so people will know how they can help.

Other materials that can help greatly are publications on various subjects for your students. You can find valuable resources from the organizations mentioned earlier that can provide magazines, books, brochures, Bible study materials, and so on. If you need money for these items, you can pursue grants available through organizations and foundations. If you're not familiar with how to apply for grants, just mention it to your parent group, and you'll probably find someone who has that knowledge and will share it with you.

The long-term response following a crisis may seem overwhelming at first when you're coming off the short-term response period. But if you remember to take one step at a time in addressing each need as it comes up, you'll see that it can be very manageable. Make sure you're accessing all resources available to you, and that will lighten your load. Keep your crisis team informed and engaged through it all.

In coming to the end of this chapter, you may realize how much you've learned about crisis response through the prevention, intervention, and "postvention" stages. But there's one more aspect your students will experience that you should consider, and that's when local or national crises occur. These definitely impact your church or school, so it would be wise to do what you can to prepare for those types of calamities. Your preparedness can mean the difference between your students feeling helpless or feeling empowered. A book on crisis response would be incomplete without discussing it.

10   LOCAL AND NATIONAL CRISES

Kids today are growing up in a harsh world. The innocence of childhood has been stolen by school tragedies, the September 2001 terrorist attacks, and natural disasters. Then, in 2004, the world was shocked by the tragedy in Beslan, Russia, with the terrorist attack that killed more than 250 children in a school. The threat is at North America's door now. It has been said that there are terrorist cells in the United States with the intent of attacking schools with the same strategy as the Beslan tragedy.[1]

Before the rash of shootings, school was one of the few safe places parents could send their children without worrying. There were incidents of bullying and conflicts with classmates, but many of those were considered growing pains to endure until graduation. Who can forget the televised images of tearful children who have been deeply impacted by a tragedy at their school?

Now our children have access to videotape footage of terrorists beheading hostages, mass graves with hundreds of bodies, and video games too gruesome for most adults. Yet I'm encouraged to see young people's humanitarian efforts in reaching out to survivors of the world's natural disasters. Even though young people have been desensitized to some extent by the media images around them, they're still idealistic about wanting to make this world a better place.

As youth workers, we must become aware of what these local and national tragedies are doing to our kids, and we must consciously target our efforts in helping them process what's coming at them. Understanding the impact on our kids can help us determine ways to equip them to deal with these tragedies.

Understanding the Impact

Often as adults we don't truly understand how local or national tragedies impact our young people. Even though our kids may say they're OK and haven't been affected, we know they *have* been affected. No one who sees a disaster is completely unaffected by it. Some students show obvious signs of trauma while others may not. Sometimes delayed reactions will occur anywhere from a few days to a few years after a tragedy. As one who works with students, you can look for some common responses to disaster:

- Disbelief and shock
- Fear and anxiety about the future
- Disorientation; difficulty making decisions or concentrating
- Inability to focus on schoolwork and extracurricular activities
- Apathy and emotional numbing
- Irritability and anger

- Extreme mood swings
- Sadness and depression
- Feelings of powerlessness
- Extreme changes in eating patterns; loss of appetite or overeating
- Crying for no apparent reason
- Headaches and stomach problems
- Difficulty sleeping
- Suspected use of alcohol and drugs[2]

In attempting to help kids, we must be careful about setting unrealistic expectations for their behavior. We must help them understand that everyone will go through the healing process at different rates, and if theirs is slower than others, that does not mean there's a problem with them. Often adults make comments such as, "You're handling this so well, better than everyone else in the youth group," or "Since you're afraid, that means you're not trusting God." We all go through natural reactions to trauma, and through time we'll be able to recover. Fear, doubt, and questioning are all a part of the healing process, and we must be careful not to shame our young people for where they are in their healing process.

God is at work in each life, and we must not get in the way or play the part of the Holy Spirit in trying to rush our students through the process before they've had the chance to truly heal. We must understand why some of our kids may be more heavily impacted than others—even within the same family. The degree of impact is based on several factors:

- Exposure: The closer a child is to the location of a

threatening and/or frightening event, and the longer the exposure, the greater the likelihood of severe distress. The length of exposure is also extended by repeated images on television, regardless of their location.

• Relationships: Having relationships with the victims of a disaster (such as those who were killed, injured, and/or threatened) is strongly associated with psychological distress. The stronger the child's relationships with the victims, the greater the likelihood of severe distress. Children who have lost a caregiver are most at risk.

• Initial reactions: How children first respond to trauma will greatly influence how effectively they deal with stress in the aftermath. Those who display more severe reactions (such as becoming hysterical or panicking) are at greater risk for the types of distress that will require mental health assistance.

• Perceived threat: The child's subjective understanding of the traumatic event can be more important than the event itself. Simply stated, severely distressed children will report perceiving the event as extremely threatening and/or frightening. Among the factors influencing children's threat perceptions are the reactions of significant adult caregivers.[3]

Understanding all these aspects of how our young people are handling traumatic experiences will help us know what they need from us. As adults, we have a lot of power, and we can help or hinder their healing process and recovery from tragedy. We aren't experts in knowing what to do in each of our student's lives, so we must remember to get help in working with our kids. Most likely you have people connected with your church or school who can help in this area if your staff is not qualified to handle some of these issues. God does not expect you to be an expert in all areas, so don't be afraid to ask for help when needed.

We can see that crisis response is serious work. Whether the crisis is in our own backyard, in a neighboring town, or across the country or world, we're all impacted to some degree. One of the most basic yet effective ways to help our students work through their issues when disaster strikes is to give them concrete ways to reach out. Let's explore some ideas for young people in response to local and national tragedies.

Local Tragedies

Several activities are appropriate for local and national crises, and many offered here can be implemented for either situation. When a tragedy occurs locally, there are more options and opportunities to help out due to the closeness in proximity. It's important to listen to news reports about the incident to find out the needs of those involved. Pray for wisdom to understand other needs that may not be so obvious.

Is there is a need for food, water, blankets, clothing, books, supplies, and so on? Your students can get involved in collection efforts. Is there a need for clean-up of debris? In that case, as many hands as possible to do the work are always a welcome sight. Is there a need to serve food? Working in a food service line can have a strong impact on kids as they see face-to-face those who have been touched by the tragedy.

Personalized outreaches can also be powerful. Creating a huge poster with your students' signatures and thoughts of well-wishes and prayers can mean a lot to those on the receiving end. Check beforehand to see if it's appropriate to make such a gesture. Making smaller cards or a book of thoughts from your group can also be an encouragement to others in a time of need.

You might adopt a church youth group or school in the area of the tragedy. It's important to contact them first to let them know your idea. Inform them if you expect anything back from them. They may hesitate to get involved in a joint effort if they think they'll have a responsibility in reaching back to you. At a later date they may be able to correspond with you, but realize that in the midst of the chaos of a crisis, they may not be open to the idea if they think there's something they may have to do in return.

Another idea that was implemented at the school where I work was something called a "Souper Bowl," designed to benefit a needy family in our school. The catering classes and the ceramics classes at our school got together to plan an event featuring ceramic bowls and soup that was patterned after a program called the "Empty Bowl Project." Our "Souper Bowl" project was slightly different, though.

People bought a ceramic bowl for $5.00 and then went to fill the bowl with soup—the ceramics classes made the bowls, and the catering classes made three types of soup. The customer also got bread, salad, and a drink. The students had received donations of bread and salad from various businesses in the community. They raised $705 for the cause, and the classes picked a club at school called the B.I.O.N.I.C. Team (which we'll discuss in the next chapter) to use the money to help a needy family in our community.

In asking the family about its needs, we were told about the sleeping arrangements of the kids in the residence. The three of them slept in the same room. The younger sister had a bed, but the two high school girls slept on the floor. We asked one of the girls what they could use most, and she said a bunk bed so each girl could sleep on a bed instead of the hard floor. The girls were so excited to get the bunk bed, and it made their Christmas very special. They beamed from ear to ear for weeks.

Here are some other ideas your kids may want to pursue to help in tragedies. Please note: if you do anything of a spiritual nature for a secular entity, make sure it's not done in a condescending way that could turn people away from God instead of toward Him.

- Prayer—by far the most important thing anyone can do
- Posters from your church, school, and so on
- E-mail messages
- Letters
- Food and drinks
- Ask a local massage therapy college to provide free chair massages.
- Ask a local pet store or animal shelter to provide puppies to hug at a student or staff gathering.

- Books and literature: If provided to a secular entity, remember to make sure not to preach at the recipients.
- Check to see if free counseling could be provided by local counseling providers.
- Open your gym or facilities as a place for youth to gather for fun activities or just to hang out together.

National Crises

For other tragedies, your group could sponsor a car wash, garage or rummage sale, bake sale, and so on to raise money for the cause. You can designate the proceeds to go to a specific purpose or give it to a reputable nonprofit organization that's participating in relief efforts. If you have a small church or school, you can even combine efforts with others in the community.

At our school, several clubs and community businesses combined efforts for garage sales for the Asian tsunami victims and then about six months later for the hurricane victims on the Gulf Coast of the United States. In case you're interested in such an effort and haven't been involved in one, here are some ideas that worked for us:

- All proceeds went to the relief efforts of the Red Cross.
- It was like a huge garage sale inside the high school cafeteria.
- People reserved a booth to sell items furnished by their student or parent group, store, church, business, and so on.
- There were booths where toys, crafts, clothes, furniture, food, books, jewelry, electronics, etc. were sold.

- The people provided all the tables and chairs for their booths.
- They listed prices on the items or left the price up to the buyer. All proceeds went to the tsunami or hurricane victims.
- Folks set up, supervised, and cleaned up their own booth areas. No items could be left after the event.
- Items from the booths were purchased at a designated check-out area.

Here's what we needed to accomplish the whole thing:

- Student or parent groups, stores, and churches to run booths where items were sold.
- Student volunteers helped with various tasks throughout the day: Elementary students were greeters and gave directions. Middle school students bagged items that were bought. High school students ran food and beverage booths.
- Adult volunteers helped supervise.
- Setup and cleanup were done by each group who reserved a booth.
- Stores donated plastic bags in which to carry items, food and beverages to sell at their own booth or a booth run by high school students (if prearranged), and other items to sell at their own booths.

The garage sales were a big success even though there were several other conflicting events on each of the days. We had different groups in charge of publicity, organizing the layout of the room, setup and take-down, registration for those wanting booths, and so on. Probably the most exciting aspect of it was seeing all those groups come together to help people in need. It had such a positive effect on the school that people were still buzzing about it a few weeks later. We raised $3,200 and $1,700 at the garage sales respectively.

Another outreach by some students following the September 11 tragedy deeply impacted a lot of people. After hearing of the children who lost loved ones in the terrorist attacks, we set out to collect stuffed animals to send to them, and the idea for "Teddies Against Terrorism" was born. We ended up collecting more than 1,400 stuffed animals to send to New York City. Here's how to go about doing something similar:

Make some calls to the areas impacted by the tragedy to determine their needs. It's best to wait a couple days after the calamity before making the calls because the immediate needs resulting from the tragedy will take precedence, and those impacted will not be able to think through how you can help them until later.

If the tragedy was at a school, you'll need to contact the school office, or the school district's office if it's within a school district. If it was a church or place of business that's still in operation and hasn't been destroyed, you can contact them directly.

Because the World Trade Center was destroyed and we heard the American Red Cross was involved, we called the American Red Cross. We also looked at the Web sites of the Red Cross and the New York State Department of Education to see which schools were impacted and similar sites to get related information. We also paid attention to the newscasts to find out what was being done.

Get an organizational team together and determine job responsibilities. We determined how we were going to run the teddy drive—through schools, churches, and places of business—and determined who would be responsible for each entity.

One student, who was in charge of schools, was a leader in his youth group and decided to ask a student from each school represented in the youth group to be the coordinator for his or her school. We had eight schools involved.

We asked the managers of two area grocery stores if we could put a collection box at the entrances of the stores. We stopped by every couple of days to get the bears from each box.

Determine the logistics for your project. *Publicity:* We knew we needed to get the word out, so we called a local printing and copying business and asked if they would donate flyers and posters. We made the flyers and posters on the computer, and they printed them.

Collection boxes: We realized that teddy bears would have to be collected at each location. We called some local moving companies and asked them to donate boxes for our drive.

Shipping: We called local radio and television stations and asked if they would help us get word out that we needed help in shipping the bears. One station gave us the name of a company that was shipping teddy bears to New York. We called them, and they let us ship our teddies with theirs. They sent 50, we sent over 1,400—and *they* paid for the shipping.

We received some exciting news that meant a lot to all the kids involved when I was at a national school counselors' conference in Florida the summer after the September 11 tragedy. At an awards banquet I sat next to a woman from New York. We began talking about their ordeal. She mentioned how much it meant for people around the world to reach out to them in so many ways.

She said, "We even had a school send us some teddy bears and stuffed animals."

I replied, "Oh, we collected and sent stuffed animals to the Red Cross in New York to give to some schools."

She said, "I wonder if those were the ones you guys sent. My favorite was a big blue teddy bear."

I paused. "We sent a big blue teddy bear, and that was my favorite too."

We stopped and looked at each other. There was no way I could trace if that was the teddy bear we sent, but I tend to believe that it was. Because we ended up sitting next to each other at a conference banquet in Florida with more than 1,000 people in attendance, I believe it was God's message of hope to both of us. She gave me a big hug and went on to tell me what happened when the kids at her schools received those teddy bears. It brought such joy to my heart. When I got home I couldn't wait to share it with the kids. We truly had made a difference, and we brought some life and happiness to hurting children on the other side of the country. That made all the work and effort worth it!

These activities were a lot of work, but also a lot of fun.

The students involved in the projects learned skills that are helping them in many other areas too. The biggest benefit to the young people, though, was knowing they brought a little happiness to others in need. In the midst of the horror and despair of seeing local and national tragedies unfold before our eyes, there's a way to combat those feelings. First, as youth workers, we must understand the depth of the hurt our kids feel in trying to sort it all out. Only then can we understand where to begin the healing process.

One of the most meaningful ways to turn tragedy around is to empower our young people to do what they can to help others in need. In the next chapter we'll discuss what one group is doing that you could do to help your youth group or school minister to others in need as well as minister to those within your own ranks. These will develop life skills in your kids that they'll use to make a difference for the rest of their lives.

HOW ONE GROUP IS MAKING
A DIFFERENCE

Young people are always eager to get behind a good
cause. They're idealistic and believe they truly can make a
difference. When a crisis occurs, kids feel helpless because
they really want to help, but often they're not given a chance
to get involved. Either they're not trained adequately, or it's
just not appropriate for youngsters to have the level of in-
volvement they desire. In the area of crisis response, one of
the best ways for kids to work through their grief is to do
something tangible to help others.

The need is great. Students have peers struggling all
around them every day, even though they may not be suffer-
ing to the degree of some of the students we've discussed in
this book. Growing up is tough, and for kids to know someone cares and is supporting them through challenging times
gives them the encouragement to keep pressing on. God is
looking for people to reach out to help those in need.

One of the side benefits of helping our young people by
equipping them with the life and ministry skills they develop

in helping others is the fact that they'll use these skills the rest of their lives. A club we started at the school where I work is doing just that, and churches and schools can adapt the idea to fit their needs too.

The Need

Because they wanted to establish ongoing methods to help struggling peers, some of the students in the school where I work met with me to discuss possibilities.

I told them about a speaker I heard when I was in high school during a district student council workshop. His name was Earl Reum. He made such an impact on me and used a phrase that inspired me. He said that society had the opinion that young people are focused only on themselves and don't care about others. He added, though, that he saw a lot of youth who really did care about making a positive impact on society.

Dr. Reum challenged us to become B.I.O.N.I.C. people. Two television shows at that time featured actors becoming bionic people with superhuman abilities because of mechanical arms, legs, eyes, and such that they received due to accidents on the job. That's not what Dr. Reum was implying with his B.I.O.N.I.C. term. He challenged us to tell society, "Believe It Or Not, I Care"—to care about treating others with respect, to care about keeping our schools clean, to care about those around us in need.

The Plan

The students liked the B.I.O.N.I.C. concept. We talked

about ways we could apply it in our school, and we pondered the idea of a club with that as the focus. We talked about the five types of students who fall through the cracks at school who often began experiencing attendance, academic, and discipline problems. These are students who—

- are new to our school
- have extended illnesses or health conditions
- are hospitalized
- lose a loved one
- experience a school tragedy

We decided to go for it and call the club the B.I.O.N.I.C. Team. The students talked with administrators about starting the club and the process to pursue it. We sat down to form a mission statement and set some goals.

Here's the mission statement: "The B.I.O.N.I.C. Team is an organization designed to help fellow students, students' families, and staff through challenging times."

The goals we set were—

- to make new students feel welcome
- to reach out to hospitalized students
- to reach out to students with extended illnesses/health conditions
- to reach out to students and their families and staff who experience the death of a loved one
- to reach out to other schools that experience tragedies

We decided to create five teams within the big team— one to address each of the club goals—and our method of reaching out to each group of students would be as follows:

- **New Student Team** to give new students a survival kit of a candy bar and a pencil with the school logo. (More recently we were given planners to add to the kit.) We also hosted a lunch each month for students who had recently joined the student body so they could get to know each other and hopefully develop some friendships.

- **Extended Illness Team** to help students who had been absent five days by sending a packet to help them organize homework assignments, information on tutors available to them, a personalized card, a letter of support, and a B.I.O.N.I.C. Team brochure.

- **Hospitalization Team** that would deliver a specially made mug with chocolates inside (or a mug and balloon for those with dietary restrictions) with a personalized card to the student in the hospital.

- **Loss Team** that would, within two weeks of the death of a loved one, deliver a pie to the home of the student's family. For staff members, we delivered the pie to them at school. For single staff members we gave a local coffee shop gift card.

- **School Tragedy Team** that created a 24-to-28-foot poster with signatures from our students and staff that would be sent to a school that had experienced a tragedy.

Next we wanted to test the waters to see how the concept would be received throughout the school. Since it was shortly before Thanksgiving, we decided to try a pie outreach to students and staff members who had lost a loved one in the previous six months. We sent word to the staff and asked for names of those students and staff.

The catering teacher said her cooking class could make the pies for us. When the number of pies grew to more than 20—beyond what the cooking class could provide—we contacted our parent booster club, and they provided the extra five pies we needed.

The Monday and Tuesday before Thanksgiving we had our work cut out for us to deliver those 25 pies. We had an incredible response to the effort, so we knew we needed to go ahead with our plans for the club. When we put in the application for the club to our administration, they said we probably couldn't use the name B.I.O.N.I.C., because it was likely copyrighted.

I contacted Dr. Reum, and he told me the story of how the B.I.O.N.I.C. acronym came into existence. He said that the student council executive committee for our district came up with that idea in 1970 as the theme for that year. He said the term was not copyrighted and that it was ours to use in whatever way we wanted. He said those students from 1970 would be so proud to know that 30 years later young people were still using "B.I.O.N.I.C." to make an impact.

We set the date for our first B.I.O.N.I.C. Team meeting. We agreed there would be a leader and assistant leader for each of the five teams and that the members could sign up for one or more or all five teams. We created a membership application form, leader application form, and brochure. We set the meeting for the main office conference room over both lunch periods on a Tuesday. That room seats 18, so we were confident we would have plenty of room.

More than 60 students showed up! We were excited by the response, but we knew we had work to do. Leaders were selected shortly after that first meeting and were trained before the next meeting.

The Results

B.I.O.N.I.C. Team meetings were held every month in order to update all the members on the outreaches of the five teams. The individual teams met together as needed, which meant twice a month early on, but once everything got rolling they met on an as-needed basis.

Because we were organizing a new club, it was necessary to create all the forms, procedures, and policies, which took a lot of time and effort.

We created B.I.O.N.I.C. Team referral boxes and put them in the most visible spots in the school for students and staff to let us know of those in need. We also set up an e-mail address for referrals and so on.

When we received a referral, the sponsor contacted the student, staff member, or family and asked for permission to do the outreach. If the people declined our offer, we did not pursue it further. If they accepted our offer, the sponsor contacted the team leader of the appropriate team. The team leader then contacted the assistant team leaders to activate the outreach.

Between Thanksgiving and the end of the school year, we were amazed by the number of outreaches we initiated. The total outreaches we performed in the first year of the club were—

- 66 new student survival kits
- 5 new student lunches
- 21 homework make-up packets for sick students
- 12 mugs and chocolates for hospitalized students
- 60 pies/coffee gift cards for students or staff who had recently lost loved ones
- 5 posters sent to other schools that experienced the death of a student
- 2 posters sent to Louisiana and Mississippi for Hurricane Katrina survivors
- 1 huge card that was sent to a school that lost a teacher.

The students became aware of other needs they wanted to address. They wanted to reach out to staff at our school to show appreciation for all they do, so they hosted a continental breakfast for the staff during the week of achievement tests and also sent a welcome card and gift to new staff members at the beginning of the year. The next year, students noticed that it had been an extremely stressful year for staff due to changes at school. The students got busy and came up with 30 donated one-hour massages and held a drawing for interested staff members.

The kids wanted to do other outreaches too, so we participated in the garage sales for the tsunami and hurricane victims, plus the "Souper Bowl" that was mentioned in chapter 10.

The support we've received from the student body, staff, and community has been very rewarding. The B.I.O.N.I.C. Team was chosen as the group out of all the clubs and activities at school to disseminate the money raised from the Souper Bowl and is evidence that our outreaches are making a difference.

We made some mistakes and learned some lessons in launching this program that may be of help to others wanting to start a similar effort.

Lessons Learned

The success of the B.I.O.N.I.C. Team has shown us how much young people really do care. Each month we have more students wanting to join the team. It's exciting to watch the students develop new skills that will serve them as they grow into adults. Often in times of difficulty youth don't know what to do or say to someone going through a tough time, so they just ignore it. The B.I.O.N.I.C. Team helps remove those fears and gives the kids practical knowledge in reaching out to others.

It was challenging to find the resources to carry out all we wanted to do. At the beginning we had nothing, and in order to start such a multifaceted club, others had to catch the vision. We needed money to buy supplies, make copies, and so on. We shared our thoughts with the parent booster club at school, and the parents got excited about the possibilities and gave us $1,500 to fund our purchase of the start-up items we needed.

We learned we needed to tweak our system of getting information on ill or hospitalized students. We often didn't hear about them until they were back at school. So we adapted our outreaches to those students to meet their unique needs.

We found that many of the students we placed in leadership had never been in leadership positions before. They were very caring kids, but they typically served behind the scenes in groups. This necessitated more leadership training than we had planned. Most of them met the challenge, but some still struggled. So we encouraged them to recruit people from their team to help in various ways. It turned out to be a great opportunity to more heavily involve those willing to play a bigger role on the team.

With five individual teams doing various outreaches, communication between all the leaders and the members became a huge undertaking. It has been a challenge to find times when all the leaders can meet. That issue hasn't been completely resolved yet, but we've instituted some other avenues to aid in the effort, such as e-mail, a glass-encased bulletin board, and a leadership retreat. We currently have more than 180 students on the B.I.O.N.I.C. Team. Getting timely information out to all students about meetings, outreaches, and so on is a continually evolving process.

We've learned that it's wise to recommend to students that they sign up for no more than three teams rather than all five. If students are involved in any other activities, five teams are just too many. If they insist they want to be on all five teams, we ask them to pick their favorite three first. If they're able to attend everything on each of those teams for a few months, we allow them to join one more team. If they can handle that, they can join the fifth.

We've discovered the importance of asking adults to help with deliveries. The loss team, hospitalization team, and school tragedy team each has its own adult volunteer to supervise deliveries. This saves the sponsor from having to supervise and participate in every delivery.

Let me close with two different stories from deliveries we've made that will show the importance of an effort like the B.I.O.N.I.C. Team. The loss team made two pie deliveries one night—one to a student who lost a grandparent and one to a student whose father had died. At the home of the student who lost her grandparent, the girl was very gracious and eloquently expressed her thanks for our act of reaching out to her and her family. When we make pie deliveries, we deliver the pie with a brief comment of our sympathy. One of the team members says the greeting. We tell the family ahead of time that we're coming and that they don't need to invite us in because we know it's a delicate time for the family, and we don't want to infringe on their privacy. If a family invites us in, we accept, though we stay for a short time.

At the second home, one of the girls on the team who had never said the greeting before asked if she could do it this time. The family asked us to come in, and after the girl greeted them, the mother burst into tears. We stayed an appropriate time and then left after lots of tears and hugs. When we finished that delivery, we all stood out by our cars to briefly process these two experiences and assess if any of us were struggling or needed support.

The girl who made the presentation at the last house said, "Ms. Austin, what did I do wrong to make the mother cry?"

I gave her a big hug and replied, "You didn't do anything wrong. The loss is very great, and that's just where the mom is right now in her process. No, you didn't do anything wrong."

This young girl had done at least five deliveries before that particular one, and no one had ever burst into tears as the mom did, so she thought she had done something wrong to cause that to happen. All of us stood and talked about it for a while as we reviewed the evening's events. The kids who were there that night will never forget the difference between those two reactions to grief. It's a life lesson that could not have been learned any other way.

Another example is of what happened with the school tragedy team. An urban school experienced the unexpected death of one of its students. Our school is suburban, with very little ethnic diversity. Our students had signed a 28-foot poster, and the two leaders and I were on our way to deliver it. The two leaders come from completely different backgrounds and would typically not have much to do with each other at school because of the groups they were in. On the way, I talked with them about what to expect at the school as it was very different from ours. When we pulled up, there were about 40 students sitting outside in front of the school. We went in, delivered the poster to the administrators, and went back to my car.

I asked the two leaders how the experience was for them. One of the leaders said, "I just looked down at my feet as I walked past all those kids, because I felt all of them staring at me like I didn't belong there."

The other said, "Ms. Austin, I just stared straight ahead to the door. I didn't look at any of them, because I was afraid they may think I'm giving a look to challenge them." Then he added, "I wonder how many students who come to our school as new students or to play us in sports feel something like that too." We talked about the experience on the way home and ways we could try to change that through what we do on the B.I.O.N.I.C. Team.

These experiences touched my heart deeply. To see my students' eyes opened to the harsh reality of our society and then explore ways they can use their lives to try to positively impact their world was powerful. It makes the hard work worthwhile. Kids really do care, and I get a front-row seat as I watch them change their world. I wouldn't trade it for anything.

More information on the B.I.O.N.I.C. Team is available at <www.restoringhopes.com>.

12	FORMS

This chapter consists of sample forms to help you as you develop your youth group or school crisis plan. First, we'll show some examples of items not in your crisis team manual. Then we'll provide a list of the forms we recommend that you include in your manual. If there's a * in front of the name of the form, there's a sample of that form in this chapter. For forms that are self-explanatory, we won't provide a sample. If you have questions about the form, you can see the descriptions of the form in chapter 3 unless otherwise indicated in parentheses. The samples can be revised to fit your needs. The forms will be presented in the order they go in your crisis team manual under the five sections listed in chapter 3: (1) Contact Information, (2) Emergency Response, (3) Planned Response, (4) Procedures/Communication, and (5) Forms/Documentation.

Before we go to the forms for the crisis team manual, we'll show a couple of resources that are not in the manual.

Crisis Team Phone Card

Crisis Team Phone Card		
Member	**Work Phone**	**Home Phone**
Jeff T.	998-555-9870	998-555-9056
Beverly J.	998-555-9872	998-555-9089
Jerome S.	998-555-9867	998-555-6534
Tommy C.	998-555-9869	998-555-4489
Sally B.	998-555-9865	998-555-3416
Simon N.	998-555-9862	998-555-5432
Brett A.	998-555-9867	998-555-5656
Tyler W.	998-555-9868	998-555-1123

Courage to Call Card (chapter 7)

The Courage to Call
Five people I can call when I'm struggling:

Name   Number

_____

_____

_____

_____

_____

Lifelines

- Pray
- Read the Bible
- Talk to a trusted adult
- Call a friend
- Listen to praise/worship music
- Write a letter to God
- Journal

You are loved!

Checklist of Forms for Your Crisis Team Manual

Front Pocket of the Manual

- ☐ Packet for Initial Crisis Team Meeting—Incident Report Form, Students/Staff Impacted by the Incident, Determining Expected Degree of Trauma, Crisis Team Member Responsibilities
- ☐ 10 Attendance Sheets
- ☐ Red/Green Card

Section 1: Contact Information

- ☐ *Crisis Contact Information
- ☐ *Other Important Numbers
- ☐ *Other Emergency Numbers
- ☐ Phone Numbers Within the Building
- ☐ Staff Work Phone Numbers
- ☐ Staff Phone Tree
- ☐ Off-Campus Staff
- ☐ Student Contact Information
- ☐ Feeder/Area Schools and Churches
- ☐ *Community Contact Numbers

Section 2: Emergency Response

- ☐ *Emergency Duties Checklist
- ☐ *Staff Members Trained in CPR and First Aid
- ☐ Accidents Near the Church/School
- ☐ Fires
- ☐ Lockdowns
- ☐ Evacuations
- ☐ Violent Intruder
- ☐ (Add other pages for emergency situations specific to your church/school/region)
- ☐ *Crisis Response Kit Checklist
- ☐ *First-Aid Checklist

Section 3: Planned Response

- ☐ *Incident Report Form
- ☐ *Students/Staff Impacted by the Incident
- ☐ *Determining Expected Degree of Trauma
- ☐ Crisis Team Member Responsibilities—Team Manager
- ☐ Crisis Team Member Responsibilities—Communications Rep
- ☐ *Crisis Team Member Responsibilities—Care-and-Concern Reps
- ☐ Crisis Team Member Responsibilities—Staff Reps
- ☐ Crisis Team Member Responsibilities—Clerical Rep
- ☐ Crisis Team Member Responsibilities—Facilities Rep
- ☐ Auxiliary Members' Duties—Parent Reps
- ☐ Auxiliary Members' Duties—Student Reps

Section 4: Procedures/Communication

- ☐ *Staff Responsibilities
- ☐ Map of the Church/School Building(s)
- ☐ Map of Evacuation Routes
- ☐ Map of Fire Drill Exit Routes
- ☐ Map of Water, Gas, and Electrical Shut-off Locations
- ☐ Meeting/Activity Calendar
- ☐ Master Schedule
- ☐ Bell Schedule
- ☐ Lunch Schedule—if you have multiple lunch periods
- ☐ *Staff Memo to Classes
- ☐ Public Address Announcements for Evacuation and Lockdown
- ☐ *Strategies for Dealing with the Media

Section 5: Forms/Documentation

- ☐ *Attendance Record
- ☐ *Students Counseled
- ☐ Impacted Students
- ☐ *Emergency Personnel Check-in Sheet

Sample Forms

Now that we've listed all the forms for your crisis team manual, you can adapt these forms for your purposes.

Sample Forms Section

Section 1: Contact Information

Crisis Contact Information

Crisis Team Members

Team Manager: _____

Communications Rep: _____

Care-and-Concern Reps: _____ and _____

Staff Reps: _____ and _____

Clerical Rep: _____

Facilities Rep: _____

Auxiliary Members: Parent Reps, _____

Auxiliary Members: Student Reps, _____

Member	Work Phone	Home Phone	Other
_____	_____	_____	_____
_____	_____	_____	_____
_____	_____	_____	_____
_____	_____	_____	_____
_____	_____	_____	_____
_____	_____	_____	_____
_____	_____	_____	_____
_____	_____	_____	_____
_____	_____	_____	_____

Other Important Numbers

John Doe_____ _____ _____

(Name)_____ _____ _____

(Name)_____ _____ _____

(Name)_____ _____ _____

(Name)_____ _____ _____

Other Emergency Numbers

Police Dept. _____

Fire Dept. _____

Ambulance/Hospital _____

Sheriff _____

State Patrol _____

Poison Control _____

Health Dept. _____

County Mental Health Agency _____

Gas/Electric Companies _____

Water Company _____

Section 2: Emergency Response

Emergency Duties Checklist

In an emergency situation, the following persons or the backups will be responsible for the following duties:

911 Caller: Will call immediately when necessary

_____ Backup _____

First-Aid Kit: Will get first-aid kit and bring it to the scene of the emergency

_____ Backup _____

Crisis Response Kit #1: Will take the kit to the designated area

_____ Backup _____

Crisis Response Kit #2: Will take the kit to the designated area

_____ Backup _____

Directing Emergency Personnel as emergency vehicles arrive on the scene

_____ Backup _____

Traffic Control: If traffic is a factor, direct traffic away from the scene. (During training of duties, consult authorities for best procedures for different scenarios.)

_____ Backup _____

Crowd Control: (If a crowd begins to gather, will keep it away from the scene.)

_____ Backup _____

Protecting the Scene: (Will protect the scene immediately for safety of all involved and keep scene undisturbed for possible police investigation)

_____ Backup _____

Staff Members Trained in CPR

Name   Position

_____   _____

_____   _____

_____   _____

_____   _____

_____   _____

_____   _____

Staff Members Trained in First Aid

Name   Position

_____   _____

_____   _____

_____   _____

_____   _____

_____   _____

Crisis Response Kit Checklist

The Crisis Response Kit is where you store important information and items you will need in the case of an evacuation from the building. It needs to be portable and easy to handle. It is recommended to have at least two crisis response kits in your building—preferably in separate parts of the building in case one area is blocked off during an emergency. Each crisis response kit should have the same items in it and needs to have a designated crisis team member and a back-up who is responsible to grab the bag during an evacuation. The crisis response kit should contain:

- Sources to use in contacting all staff members—a staff roster including work, cell, and home phone numbers, addresses, etc.
- A student directory of student and parent phone numbers, addresses, etc.
- Important community phone numbers—emergency services numbers (police, fire, hazardous materials clean-up, etc.), utility companies, area businesses, medical entities (hospitals, clinics, etc.), area churches, area schools, etc.
- Class lists
- Master schedule
- Copies of student and staff health records
- Blueprints of the building including emergency shut-off valves for gas, electricity, water, etc.
- Pens, pencils, markers
- Paper, writing tablets
- Flashlight
- First-aid kit
- Master keys to the building
- A copy of the crisis team manual
- Other items deemed necessary

First-Aid Kit Checklist

There are many recommendations for what needs to be in a first-aid kit. The following list gives you some ideas of where to begin:

- Band-Aids
- instant ice packs
- hydrogen peroxide
- rubbing alcohol
- tweezers
- aspirin or nonaspirin medication, such as Tylenol (for only you or other adults—don't give to students without written permission)
- surgical (latex) gloves
- thermometer (the small, plastic disposable ones are handy)
- antibiotic ointment or cream (such as Neosporin)
- antibacterial or antiseptic spray (such as Bactine)
- bug bite cream or lotion (such as Cortaid or Cortizone 10)
- gauze
- medical tape
- You may also need to keep a biohazard kit on hand in case of bleeding (available in janitorial supply catalog or visit <www.safetyonline.com> for links to suppliers). In addition to surgical gloves and medical supplies, you'll need a chemical that absorbs blood spills and sanitizes the area. If you need a more extensive medical kit (remote location, international travel, special-needs kits), consult with trained medical personnel.[1]

Section 3: Planned Response

Incident Report Form

Date _____

Persons involved _____

Incident _____

Where _____

When _____

Parents/Guardians _____

Home situation—lives with: both parents/one parent/grandparent/

other _____

Siblings   Age   Grade   School

_____

_____

_____

_____

_____

Details of the incident _____

_____

_____

_____

_____

Confidential information not to be shared ouside the crisis team

_____

_____ 4

Determining Expected Degree of Trauma

Step 1: Circle the number(s) in each triangle beside any word or phrase that describes this death. Total the circled numbers within each triangle.

Step 2: Add the triangle totals. Then add one point for each additional person who died or was critically injured in this event to determine a GRAND TOTAL: _____

A. WHO

STUDENT
- Popular/well known (6)
- Other (3)

TEACHER/OTHER STAFF
- Popular/well known (4)
- Under 32 years old (2)
- Not well known (1)

Total=_____

B. HOW

Murder/Suicide (6)
Accident (3)
Natural Causes:
- Unexplained (4)
- Short-term illness (3)
- Long-term illness (2)

Total=_____

C. WHERE

At school (4)

Local community (2)

Other (1)

Total=_____

Degree of Trauma

12+	High
6-11	Moderate
0-7	Low

Note: Ratings based on grand total[2]

Crisis Team Member Responsibilities

Care-and-Concern Reps

Date	Task	Member Responsible	Follow-up Needed?
	If applicable, designate a point person for ongoing communication with outside mental health support agencies.		
	Help the team manager identify resources needed for the crisis.		
	Discuss with team manager which staff members who need to be personally contacted by him or her before the voice mail announcement.		
	If requested, help the team manager plan the staff briefing/meeting.		
	Help identify staff members who will need extra support, and follow up with them periodically. (See "Staff Members and Students Who May Be Affected")		
	Help identify students who may be particularly affected by this crisis. (See "Staff Members and Students Who May Be Affected")		

Date	Task	Member Responsible	Follow-up Needed?
	Help dispel rumors.		
	Establish places where students and staff can go for support. Room _____ Facilitator _____ Room _____ Facilitator _____ Room _____ Facilitator _____		

Section 4: Procedures/Communication

Staff Responsibilities

- Keep the television and radio off during a crisis to minimize student trauma and reduce post-traumatic stress disorder symptoms. Resume normal activity as much as possible. (Y/S)
- Listen to students. (Y/S)
- Adjust curriculum or testing schedule as needed. (Y/S)
- Engage the group/class in constructive activities relating to the event. (Y/S)
- Keep accurate attendance records. (S)
- Attend all staff meetings. (Y/S)
- Announce what has happened in the group/classroom if necessary. If the leader/teacher is uncomfortable making the announcement, contact a member of crisis team for assistance. (Y/S)
- Dispel rumors. (Y/S)
- Help identify students who need counseling, both short- and long-term, and refer those students to the counseling department or other appropriate location. (Y/S)
- Have very distraught students escorted to the counseling office or other appropriate location, or call for an adult escort if needed. (Y/S)
- Give to a crisis team member a list of students and or staff who were close to the student(s). (Y/S)
- Be aware of staff members who are showing signs of distress, and notify a crisis team member. (Y/S)
- Monitor yourself and others. Seek help as needed. (Y/S)
- Attend final debriefing. (Y/S)

Memos/Letters

Sample Statement for Initial Announcement

Note: As previously mentioned, it's recommended that statements be read to the students by a teacher in the classroom setting rather than over the public address system. This allows adults to make immediate connections with students and assess whether individuals need special attention.

Example

We are sad to announce that we have learned that one of our students [staff], _____(name)_____, was involved in a serious accident [has died]. This is all the information we have at this time. We realize this is a shock to many of you, and trained counselors will be available for any students or staff who would like to talk about it or feel the need for support. We will announce shortly the location and times where you can speak with the counselors.

We ask at this time that students remain in their classrooms and attend their regularly scheduled classes. We will announce any new information as it becomes available and _____(name's)_____ family gives us permission to share it.

Attendance Record

Date _____ Time/Period _____

Teacher Name _____ Room _____

Name	Missing Before Building Evacuation	Missing After Building Evacuation	Parent Signature for Release of Student to Parent

Strategies for Dealing with Media

Be Prepared

- Have individual school and district fact sheets prepared.

- Identify a communication center and a separate media briefing area for each campus (this should be done together with the principal and the head of school security).

- Pick the media briefing area carefully:
  - Do not pick the area based on a site map
  - The area should be easily accessible to the media
  - The area should *not* give the media immediate and/or easy access to the campus.

- The communication center is where all internal information flows to and from.

- Make site maps of all your schools once the communication center and media briefing areas are chosen, making sure each is clearly marked on the site map.

- Distribute the maps to educational teams.

- Meet with the media spokespersons from your local police and fire departments and, if you are near a military installation, the public affairs officer there. Review your plan and site maps so they know where to go and so they'll know who you are and will be more likely to stay in contact with you during a crisis. Establishing rapport with those teams is very important.

- Identify your school/crisis spokesperson and do not change your choice. If you have a public relations office, it should handle this duty, because it frees up school personnel, and that office has access to pertinent school information.

- If possible, individual school personnel should not speak with the media.

- In a crisis situation and after the original media release is completed, the media should be updated every half-hour for the first two hours and then hourly thereafter, even if it means telling them there's nothing new to report.

- Later briefings should contain information regarding steps the school will be taking the following day, such as checking school bags, increased police presence, need to show ID, and so on.

- Since a recent poll noted that more than 65 percent of Americans get their news from television, prepare your media releases for television broadcast. If a crisis occurs at your school, the majority of parents will watch television news that night for information.

- Try to be in the media briefing room before the media arrive in the morning. If there's no news, it's a good opportunity to note your district's concern for the safety of the students, review steps being taken to secure the campus, and so on, plus the district's record for having safe schools. These reports will make noon news because you've established yourself as the only source of news until students come.

- Understand that the media needs a story. Let it be a controlled, child-focused story that will help restore the safety and security of the children.[3]

Section 5: Forms/Documentation

Emergency Attendance Sheet

Teacher Name _____ Room _____

Date _____ Time/Period _____

Name	Absent from Class	Missing After Building Evacuation	Released to Parent (Time)	Notes

Students/Staff Impacted by the Incident

Students

Name   Grade   Comments

_____

_____

_____

_____

_____

_____

_____

_____

_____

_____

_____

Staff

Name   School Position

_____

_____

_____

_____

_____

_____

_____

_____

_____

Students Counseled

Date_____

Crisis Responder (Please Print) _____

Time in   Time out   Name   Grade   Comments

_____

_____

_____

_____

_____

_____

_____

_____

_____

_____

_____

_____

_____

_____

_____

_____

_____

_____

_____

_____

Crisis Responder Check-in Sheet

Date_____

Name	Agency	Supervisor	Phone #

NOTES

Chapter 5

1. Elisabeth Kübler-Ross, *On Death and Dying* (New York: Simon & Schuster, 1997).

2. "Helping Children and Teens Cope with Trauma," Colorado Organization for Victim Assistance, <www.coloradocrimevictims.org>.

Chapter 6

1. Sandy J. Austin, *Angry Teens and the Parents Who Love Them* (Kansas City: Beacon Hill Press of Kansas City, 2002), 11.

2. Dina O'Shea Robke, "What Parents Can Do in Suicide Prevention," oral presentation, Thornton, Colo., June 2006.

3. "Overcoming Compassion Fatigue," *Family Practice Management,* April 2000, <www.aafp.org/fpm/FPMprinter/20000400/39over.html?print=yes>.

4. Ibid.

5. Ibid.

Chapter 10

1. John Giduck, *Terror at Beslan: A Russian Tragedy with Lessons for America's Schools* (Golden, Colo.: The Archangel Group, 2005).

2. "Coping with Disaster," National Mental Health Association, <www.nmha.org/reassurance/youngadults.cfm>.

3. "Identifying Seriously Traumatized Children: Tips for Parents and Educators," National Association of School Psychologists, <http://nasponline.org/NEAT/psycht_general.html>.

Chapter 12

1. Ginny Olson, Diane Elliot, and Mike Work, *Youth Ministry Management Tools* (Grand Rapids: Zondervan Publishing House, 2001), 216.

2. Martha Oates, *Death in the School Community: A Handbook for Counselors, Teachers, and Administrators* (Alexandria, Va.: American Counseling Association, 1993), 21. Reprinted with permission. No further reproduction permitted without written permission from the American Counseling Association.

3. "Suggestions for Dealing with the Media," National Association of School Psychologists, <http://nasponline.org/NEAT/neat_mdia.html>.

RECOMMENDED RESOURCES

Books

Austin, Sandy. *Angry Teens and the Parents Who Love Them.* Kansas City: Beacon Hill Press of Kansas City, 2002.

Dobson, James. *When God Doesn't Make Sense.* Wheaton, Ill.: Tyndale House Publishers, 1993.

Garbarino, James. *Lost Boys: Why Our Sons Turn Violent and How We Can Save Them.* New York: Anchor Books, 1999.

Giduck, John. *Terror at Beslan: A Russian Tragedy with Lessons for America's Schools.* Golden, Colo.: The Archangel Group, 2005.

Hancock, Jim, and Rich Van Pelt. *The Youth Worker's Guide to Helping Teenagers in Crisis.* Grand Rapids: Zondervan Publishing House, 2005.

McDowell, Josh. *The Disconnected Generation: Saving Our Youth from Self Destruction.* Nashville: Word Publishing, 2000.

————. *Youth Ministry Handbook: Making the Connection.* Nashville: Word Publishing, 2000.

Mueller, Walt. *Understanding Today's Youth Culture.* Wheaton, Ill.: Tyndale House Publishers, 1999.

Oates, Martha. *Death in the School Community: A Handbook for Counselors, Teachers, and Administrators.* Alexandria, Va.: American Counseling Association, 1993.

Olson, Ginny, Diane Elliot, and Mike Work. *Youth Ministry Management Tools.* Grand Rapids: Zondervan Publishing House, 2001.

More than a Matter of Trust: Managing the Risks of Mentoring. Washington, D.C.: The Nonprofit Risk Management Center, 1998.

Pipher, Mary. *Reviving Ophelia: Saving the Selves of Adolescent Girls.* New York: Ballantine Books, 1994.

Pollack, William. *Real Boys.* New York: Henry Holt and Company, 1998.

Stanley, Charles. *When Tragedy Strikes.* Nashville: Nelson Books, 2004.

Wolfelt, Alan D. *Healing a Grieving Teen's Heart.* Ft. Collins, Colo.: Companion Press, 2001.

Yancey, Philip. *Where Is God When It Hurts?* Grand Rapids: Zondervan Publishing House, 1997.

Organizations and Associations

Organizations and publications with information for youth that can be found on the Web:

- Barefoot Ministries
- *Breakaway* Magazine
- *Brio* Magazine
- Campus Crusade for Christ
- *Campus Life* Magazine
- *Devo* Magazine
- Focus on the Family
- *Group* Magazine
- Remuda Ranch
- Teen Challenge
- Young Life
- Youth for Christ
- *Youth Specialties*
- Youth with a Mission

School and counseling organizations that can provide assistance:

- American Association of Christian Counselors
- American Association of Christian Schools
- American School Counselor Association
- Association of Christian Schools International
- Christian Schools International
- National Association of School Psychologists
- National Association of School Social Workers
- National Mental Health Association
- National Organization of Victims Assistance
- Network of International Christian Schools

Other Contacts for Crisis Issues

- American Red Cross
- Federal Emergency Management Agency (FEMA)
- The Nonprofit Risk Management Center

117695